Light The Fuse

Vincent Vargas

Light The Fuse

Editor: Kendra Middleton Williams
Book Layout & Design: Andy Grachuk - www.JingotheCat.com

Contents

Editor's Note   6

Foreword by Jocko Willink   9

Chapter 1 - Transition-The Inevitable   19

Chapter 2 - Transition-The Veteran Conundrum   31

Chapter 3 - The Asshole In The Mirror-Self-   49
            Accountability

Chapter 4 - Who The Fuck Am I? Identity   71

Chapter 5 - Motivation-Direction   87

Chapter 6 - Balance   99

Chapter 7 - Fear   115

Chapter 8 - Acceptance   127

Chapter 9 - Competition   143

Chapter 10 - Gratitude-Humility-Death   157

Post-Scripts   181

Acknowledgements   191

Note From The Editor

I t's a rare thing when I see something entirely new in my line of work. Taking on a project that will both challenge and delight me, is a true gift. When Vince commissioned me to edit this work, I had no idea what I would be taking on in terms of the unique challenges it presented. As a seasoned veteran of this industry, I love a new challenge. We worked through the preliminary edits and determined that there was a lot of work left to be done. Vince rose with eagerness to face a challenge he had never faced, writing a structured book.

I had never worked with this facet of dyslexia before now, and it was incredibly interesting to see where he would overlap one thought, before completing the last. You will see most of the text is directly from Vince's head, and the rest is what he would speak and describe to me. I put it down, deciphering the thoughts he already had on the page, but with the verbal context he provided to me. The entire process was creative and interesting, trying to help him best communicate the incredible story living inside him. Having to do rewrites and revisions on demand was a new process for Vince, and he met it like a champ. Having a disability such as dyslexia doesn't have to preclude anyone from telling the incredible stories they possess. I'm grateful he asked me to be his help with this incredible work. I hope you all enjoy reading it as much as I enjoyed helping Vince put it together.

Within the chapters, you will find various poems, blog entries, and journal entries. These are exclusively Vince's work, left completely untouched by me, save for a minor spell check. The poetry is free-form, so his pauses and exhales are delineated by line breaks and punctuation. I didn't change some of the grammar with the deliberate intent of not altering his writer voice more than necessary. We took care to keep the voice of Vince, steady throughout the book. So, if you find slang or American colloquialisms, consider it part of his organic prose. Thank you, for giving this new format of writing a chance.

Foreword

by Jocko Willink

Do you know where you are going?

Most people don't.

Even if you do know where you are going, do you know the path to get there?

Most people don't.

That's because the path taken through life is different for everyone.

It's confusing. It's filled with obstacles and obstructions.

It's filled with temptation and pain.

It's filled with sorrow and death.

Of course, there is joy and happiness. But they often come at a cost.

There is a price to be paid.

Now.

I wish I could give you directions down the path.

I wish I could tell you which way to go.

But I can't.

No one can.

There is no roadmap, no grid reference.

You are going to hit those obstacles and those obstructions.

And, while you can get some help and you can get some guidance, ultimately, it is you that have to walk the path.

Alone.

And you will have to find your own way.

But: If you open your mind and pay attention to those that have gone before you, you can find your own way a little easier.

In my old job in the military, I ended up as the commander of what is known as Training Detachment One, or TRADET-1. This was an incredible job. I was in charge of the training for the west coast SEAL Teams. This wasn't the training that is seen on TV with guys running around with boats on their heads or carrying logs or doing long-distance conditioning runs. The training I ran is where SEALs learn to shoot, move, and communicate. It is where

SEALs learn to close with and destroy the enemy. And it is where SEAL leaders learn to lead.

We at TRADET-1 went through great lengths to make the training as realistic as possible. We utilized paintball and Simunition rounds to simulate combat. We also used a multimillion-dollar laser-tag system that mounted on our actual weapons. We had Hollywood set designers fabricate and decorate our training sites so they looked like villages and cities in Iraq and Afghanistan. We even hired actors and actresses to play the roles of Arabic or Pashtun speaking locals. On top of that, we utilized pyrotechnical special effects to simulate detonating Improvised Explosive Devices, mortars, and Rocket Propelled Grenades. Finally, we employed fake blood and moulage to simulate traumatic combat casualties like the ones that are found on real battlefields.

Utilizing all those assets, we unleashed total mayhem on the SEAL Platoons we put through training. We tried to throw every possible scenario we could at the platoons: downed men, wounded men, split forces, downed vehicles, suicide bombers, barricaded enemy shooters, wounded civilians, hostages, false walls, and every other problem we could possibly think of.

But we couldn't think of everything. There was not, nor will there ever be, a way to predict exactly what will happen on the battlefield. The battlefield will always have an element that is completely random and erratic. So our goal was to show the SEAL platoons as many worst-case scenarios as we could. When the platoons would get overseas, they might not run into the exact same scenarios, but they had developed pattern recognition: they knew in a broad sense what type of bad events could unfold and how they could handle those events.

While the scenarios they would end up facing overseas would not completely match the ones they had seen in training, they understood how to apply the tactics, techniques, and procedures they learned in training, which would allow the SEAL platoons to overcome any scenario they faced. Seeing some version of a challenge before actually facing it is a game changer—it is almost an unfair advantage.

For example: take any puzzle, any riddle, or any trial, or test. Those challenges will be infinitely easier to solve if the person has seen it, or something similar to it, before. This is true in sports, in academics, in business, and of course, in combat as well.

Often times, even just reading about a combat situation can give a trooper on the ground an advantage. For instance, I remembered reading that during the Vietnam war, supposedly friendly locals that worked on American bases in Vietnam often gave intelligence to the enemy.

As it turned out, during my first deployment to Iraq, there were local Iraqi contractors working inside my compound, delivering food , clearing away waste, and providing some basic cleaning services. Call me paranoid, but having read what local civilians working in a similar capacity had done in Vietnam, we shut down our compound to the local contractors. A few weeks later some of the Iraqi contractors on another base were caught with GPS's that had important positions on the base marked—obviously to be passed onto rocket or mortar teams.

During the Battle of Ramadi in 2006, my SEAL Task Unit integrated with conventional forces as they pushed through the city, clearing it of insurgents. This was not a standard SEAL or Special Operations mission, but we took what we had learned during our training and applied it to the situation with powerful results. In both of these cases, and during all my overseas deployments, I had never trained or read about the exact situation that I would be in. But I was able to look at what we were actually facing, utilize pattern recognition, and adapt our methodologies to the emerging situation each time. Knowledge is the most powerful weapon on the battlefield.

This book by Vince "Rocco" Vargas is not just about combat. It is about life—and not a perfect life. The life Vince has been through has its own share of worst-case scenarios. It tells the story of a life filled with trials and tribulations, slings and arrows, and blunders and mistakes.

And yet, with each humbling defeat, Vince finds a way out. He discovers a way to learn and grow. He uncovers a way to become better from his errors and misfortunes. Both Vince and I learned to recognize threats, situations, and patterns from the training we went through as members of the military, from the books we read on the subject of war, and finally from the stories that were passed down from those that went before us. This book will do the same for life: allow some level of pattern recognition. It will teach the reader to see some of the mistakes that Vince made along the way so that the reader can avoid making those same mistakes.

But even if the mistakes aren't avoided, a person can still learn from this book by reading and understanding how Vince overcame these mistakes , regrouped, reorganized, and became a better person himself, eventually ending up where he is now: a successful businessman and entrepreneur, a respected family man, and promising actor.

Like the man himself, Vince's writing is raw and powerful. His journal and blog entries paint a picture of struggle and of pain. His explanations of what he went through and how he got through his struggles are not only good reading—they are also solid, straightforward advice that can be put to use immediately.

While his stories revolve around his experiences in the Army, as he puts it, they aren't only "veteran issues," instead they are "humanity issues." Yes: Anyone from any walk of life can learn from what Vince has written.

This is proven in some of his commentary, which translates perfectly from the military to the civilian world. He talks about "identifying that you are the threat," and that you need to "initiate self-rescue." Clearly, those are military terms, but they make obvious sense no matter what a person's vocation is: You are the problem, so FIX IT.

There is also a section where Vince breaks down the "Five Stages of the Veteran Transition Evolution." Of course, Vince states that "not all veterans go through all of these," and he is right. My transition from the military was different from what Vince went through and what he writes about in this book. But I did see many veterans I know go through something similar to what Vince describes. Unfortunately, they did not know what was happening—they did not recognize the storm that surrounded them. But how could they recognize it if they had not seen it before? Again, that is one of the most valuable things about Vince's book: it provides perspective. So, while Vince's description might not match exactly what any specific veteran goes through, just seeing his perspective can give a veteran, or anyone going through a major transition in life, some frame of reference, some guidance of what a person might run into, so they can avoid some of the pitfalls and get on the right path.

The book is also entertaining: "My body-type is the kind where you can tell I work out here and there, but I also never said no to a taco." He also describes the most "intimate moment in his life," occurring not in a bedroom, but in a cellblock when he was working as a prison guard and was the member of a team assigned to get control of an unruly prisoner serving a life sentence for murder. Vince had to get control of him, not with a gun or a non-lethal weapon, but with good old-fashioned fisticuffs. While Vince did defend himself and get the upper hand, it was a level of vulnerability that Vince had never dealt with.

And that is what this book is: a combination of vulnerability and good, old-fashioned fisticuffs—it is a scrap. It is a fight to get on the right path. To get to the other side. A fight to be better.

Light the Fuse by Vince "Rocco" Vargas isn't going to make you into a perfect person.

It isn't going to solve your problems for you.

But it can guide you. It can show you some mistakes to avoid.

It can show you how to recover and get back on the path if you slip off.

No one can tell you exactly how to get through life.

No can explain how to overcome the specific fight you will face.

But Vince's book can give you an advantage.

It can give you some pattern recognition so you can identify the issues in your life and overcome them.

Now go make yourself better.

Chapter One

Transition - The Inevitable

I'm Nothing Special - By Vincent Vargas

I get nervous sometimes that I'll be a role model to others.

Even that sentence makes me feel like an asshole.

I just don't want to let anyone down.

But despite that fear, I have come to the realization that my path in this life is to help others. Help others transition from active duty. Help my family and kids have a better life. Put myself out there to help others feel comfortable.

I do it willingly, but that doesn't mean it's easy.

I'm nothing special. I'm a man with insecurities just like the next.

I'm not a great man, but I try to be a good man.

And like any man – good or bad – I fail.

Often.

But I bounce back.

Life isn't easy. Obviously. One photo on social media doesn't reflect the hundreds of hours working your ass off to get to that exact moment. The funny thing is, when we reach that specific moment we want to capture, we immediately falsify it through filters, enhanced lighting, etc.

That's why when I post a selfie with my wife, I also post the other 37 pictures it took to get to that point.

THAT is the real shit. THAT is life. The highs, the lows and all the bullshit in between.

Ultimately, it doesn't really matter whether I'm viewed as a role model or not. In fact, there's a lot of shit I've done that I hope anyone reading this never does!

I guess the point of it all is to just keep going. Keep trying. Keep moving. Keep failing.

As long as you keep moving forward, that's all that matters.

I hope I can live up to the person you think I am. I am sure I'll fall short, and you won't agree with me from time to time. But the fact is I'm just a dude trying to get through life and leave a legacy behind for my kids to appreciate.

I am you, living breathing, failing and insecure...

I am you, winning, growing, learning and doubting...

We can and will get through it...

#IMakeItWeMakeIt

This sentiment is honest. This is what I envision.

If I make it, we all make it. Why? Because we are all the same. Same opportunities, same issues, same insecurities. We just have to keep moving.

When I "MAKE" it, we all do. I can hire more, I can inspire more, and I can open more doors and bridge the gaps.

Note: This is a blog I posted in May 2016. I had just booked this new TV gig and I was excited beyond words. So much goes through a man's mind when he is under the gun and feeling the muzzle. Wondering if we would make it to production and whether or not I would be able to pay my bills until then. So much to consider all at once and I knew deep in my soul that no matter what, I would make it work. This was what I had been working so hard to achieve. This is the first huge stepping stone to the career I really want to have. I will make it. Come what may, despite all the fear and anxiety, I knew I would push through anything to make it happen.

Life is Transition

People have trouble in the struggle with transition for reasons I will never understand. It's the uncomfortable idea of change. But when you break it down, it's all we do as adults and as humans. As babies we learn so many firsts and transition to the next stage of development without stopping. We learn how to crawl, and then we transition from crawling to walking. From there, it's a transition from walking to running, playing, dribbling a ball, and on it goes. All we do in life essentially, is transition.

We put the victim's mentality behind something we do on a daily basis as human beings and we start demonizing what it is. And this is the problem. We demonize a natural behavior in an act of self-sabotage, disguised as self-preservation. It doesn't make any sense when you consider it.

I had played baseball since I was four years old, all the way up through age twenty-two. Every winter and every summer, year-round for almost eighteen years, I was playing baseball. To say I was institutionalized is an understatement; this game was really the only thing I knew as a young adult. If you asked me what was important in life, I would tell you baseball first. Everything else always came after, in no particular order. All I cared about was playing the game, this beautiful impossible puzzle.

Baseball is an impossible sport to be 'great' in, no matter how much you practice. It's in the numbers. 'Great' in the baseball world is a thirty-percent success rate. One of the places I believe my resilience comes from is years of loss in baseball.

There is one game that sticks in my memory. I remember running onto the field from the bullpen, coming in to close the game and give my team the win. A lot of trust was put on me to finish the game out, and within two batters I would have a man on first and second. At this point I would be stressing. I felt like I couldn't throw a strike no matter what I did. The harder I tried, the more I missed. The stress was getting to me. Wiping the sweat from my eyes, I threw the next pitch. I remember so clearly the moment my neck was whipped back as I tried to follow the path of the ball as it blasted past me, and the opposing team erupting in cheers. I just melted away into my dugout before the runner had even crossed the plate. I had lost games before, but this one held the embarrassment that was almost enough to retire an early career.

By far, my biggest loss was the day I knew this game was over for me. I mean this in the sense that my options for going professional had all but evaporated. To this day, I have papers from my days in kindergarten saying 'I want to play professional baseball.' I wrote a poem in the third grade that all the stars in the sky were lost homers from some of the greats who had played the game. When I was in high school, I had my baseball autograph all figured out. I would sign it so that it was just crazy enough to look cool, but clear enough to see the V in the first name and the V in my last name.

Baseball was everything to me. The show, the dream, the chase, all of it was now over.

To be completely honest, I believe I drank more after that transition than I did after my military transition. I didn't have very many responsibilities. I just had a child, but she was in California and I was in Kentucky. I knew I needed to find a way to provide for her and the baseball dream was no longer an option because of a failing grade I received in ceramics. Ceramics. It wasn't the assignments I was failing, it was the fact I didn't make it into class to turn them in. I would get them done and have them ready as assigned in the syllabus. I just stupidly didn't prioritize getting the completed work turned in when it was due. I didn't show up. I was prioritizing playing baseball and drinking beer. I wasn't able to charm my way into a C or even a D to get the 2.0 GPA required to stay eligible for athletics, and was summarily released from the team.

The simple balance of shaping a figure from dirt. I lost

my dream to a class that bears very little weight in life. Something that seemed so inconsequential but actually had the power to alter the entire course of my life. It made me feel stupid to have failed such an easy class. Especially knowing it was now all over because of my gross lack of respect for that discipline of my college education. It was practically a metaphor for what was to become of me, having to shape a man out of nothing but broken dreams.

I drank, and drank, and drank some more, believing somehow an idea that was better than baseball would come to fruition. But nothing happened. I just lived in a steady state of drunk or hungover, and broke.

I was in a bar speaking to an older gentleman named Jim one night after work. This was a typical engagement for him and me. We worked together at Texas Road House. He and a group of others were the closest thing to family I had in Kentucky. It seemed like these people were all the family I had at the time. It wasn't my finest hour.

Most nights, after a long shift, we all headed to Buffalo Wild Wings and had a few beers. It was actually kind of cool walking into the bar and Jared the bartender would ask if I wanted the 'usual.' I had a 'usual.' It made me almost feel important. Jim was in the Navy when he was younger, and we tended to have some serious conversations while drinking our beers and watching TV. I was telling him at the time that home did not feel like home anymore for me. The problem was, Kentucky was not my home either.

We were watching the news when the young Marine was putting the flag over the Saddam Hussein statue, and his family was being interviewed by CNN. They looked so proud of their son and it showed on their faces. This was the first time I realized my family has never looked that proud of me, ever. I realized I wanted desperately to make them proud of me. I owed it to them to do more than drink at a bar until I was out of money and return to work only to repeat the same cycle the next day. Not to mention, I had a daughter that I didn't have money to provide for.

This was my motivation to join the military. I had to find a new mission in life. I needed to forget baseball. It was time to forget all the time and effort I had put into the sport. I had to let the dream die and start a new one. Of course, I mourned the death of my life's work, but it wasn't helping me in my new life. It was time to transition to the next phase.

This decision wasn't an easy one. There was a small chance baseball could continue for me overseas, but I wouldn't be allowed to bring my daughter if I went. And just like that, I accepted my decision to move on to something new to improve my life.

I wasn't so much worried about dying, as much as I

was worried about not being good at my new job in the military. I signed the contract for Ranger Selection called RIP, or Ranger Indoctrination Program. That moment of thinking, 'I want to make my father proud' was now staring me in the face, and I didn't know if I was strong enough mentally and physically to not quit. I had never been tested that way, up to this point. The hardest physical activity I had ever done before that was Hell week in football. Now I was doing physical shit that was ten times harder than any of those sport days. And with success, it could lead me to a more severe consequence. Imagine that. Have we ever thought deeply about this? The harder you train your body in the military, the more your chances increase for being faced with death. That's a mind fuck.

I didn't know it in the moment that my life's path into the US Army would be the change needed to eventually be assigned to the Ranger Regiment. I would go on to earn my Ranger Tab, and be sent on three combat deployments. The decision to join originally just held the intention to afford providing my child with a decent living. But now, it has been the single most impactful transition in my life that had later lead to many other meaningful decisions. Becoming a Drill Sergeant, working with Special Operations in Corrections Department, joining Special Operations in the Border Patrol, finding success in business and entertainment, and to this very moment writing a book, all spun from my one decision to join the Army.

Maybe the scariest transitions lead to the most enriching opportunities. I was a failed college athlete. I didn't have vision for anything past that. Once I was backed into a corner I had to make a change and that change has lead to many more opportunities of transition that I now welcome.

Fighting it will not get you anywhere, while rising for it will take you everywhere. I know this from my years of resisting simple things as change and transition; you can't just wish for it, you need to also work for it. And the sad reality is that you don't get to see the actual hard work I put in to these endeavors. You just see the results, the funny jokes in a YouTube video, or the guy playing a motorcycle club member on TV. The hard work doesn't even make the 'B' roll. I sometimes wish it would.

You can't fight the rising tides, or the winds of change. But you can be lifted by the rising tide, and harness the wind in the sails. Fair winds and following seas will be our vehicle to peace. Or so I've heard, anyway. What could it hurt to try? If it doesn't challenge you, it won't change you. I have never been afraid of challenges, so why was I fighting this one so hard? I have to live with some level of faith that good things will happen with a measure of belief and willingness to show up and do the work.

Here I was showing up to a bar to get into a state that was the polar opposite of sober. I was investing no time in trying to better myself, nor my situation. It wasn't changing because I wasn't challenging myself. I was letting life hang by the chandelier, out of my reach. It seemed to escape my notice that all I needed to do was get the fuck up off the bar stool and reach for the damn thing. I have to thank my creator and my parents' raising, for finally gathering the sense to do it. I will never forget the sense of fear of that transition that I felt when I finally did drag my idiot ass up off that stool. Again, my parents showed up in me, and I summoned my intestinal fortitude to just do it and face the fear of the transition staring me down. I will never be able to fully articulate my gratitude to them.

Chapter Two

Transition - The Veteran Conundrum

Kill My Old Man - By Vincent Vargas

It has all been a lie, you tell me to believe...

You slowed me down, you said I couldn't do it...

You told me to be tough and to suck it up...

You said don't show fear that's not what men do...

You are never going to be great so just settle for the status quo...

You made me believe I wasn't worth more so I shouldn't try more...

You lied to me...

Fuck you, fuck your false hopes and dreams you said I could only imagine but can never make come to fruition.

I did it, I did it by ignoring your voice, I did it by staying the course...

I knew there was more to life and only found that once I stopped listening to you...

I can be great, I can do more and definitely am worth more...

It was so easy for you to tear me down but not any more...

I have found my voice as it washed up on shore...

Those waves of lies have proven to be weaker then my drive...

You are dead to me...

I have shot through the lies

And I have drowned out the noise

I have stabbed through the doubt

I have suffocated your voice

And buried you deeper than six feet beneath my consciousness...

I killed my old man who filled me with doubt.

I am a new man, I AM FREE I am NOW a NEW version of ME!

Note- This poem was written as my reaction to reading a quote by Henry David Thoreau. The quote is, "The mass of men lead lives of quiet desperation." It is relevant because people are so often silently afraid of so many things. They are afraid of change, transition, loss, humiliation, myriad things that are all part of life and growth in it. But most people sit quietly back in safety just desperately hoping something great will happen upon them as opposed to going and getting it. People as a rule have some type of struggle with going out and seizing the moment to get what they want. They feel safer with their desires and dreams left unknown and living a life they don't even really want, due to fear of failure.

The word transition to veterans is this seemingly scary thing that causes instant panic. They know it's coming but nobody ever actually wants to jump in and do it. I believe it is mainly because we have seen plenty of people fail and fail again, behind us. When the truth is, transition is nothing more than the taking of a breath, or the next step, walking out the door, or waking up. The first obstacle and transition of every day is waking up. Getting out of bed is the first fight of the day. It's just a transition from sleeping to waking up. It really is just a simple concept. And so, if we can stop supporting the idea that transition is hard, we can stop putting the demon, or the Boogey Man, or just the negative connotation, on the concept of transition

People should be excited for a new road or a new mission. They should not look at it as something that could potentially beat them down. And really, a failure of a transition is nothing but another transition of another transition, right? So, it's pretty simple if you break it down that way. Veterans tend to have the worst trouble with transitioning. No one person actually knows why the world wants to make it seem like every veteran can't figure out how to get out of the military. I think part of that is because everyone tells them it's going to be hard. And so, they go at it believing it's hard and making the mistake of allowing every mistake that they have ever made to be the reason why the transition is hard.

Society is more focused on the negative parts of transition than the positive. Currently we see society focused on the difficulties of transitioning to civilian life. The phrase 'twenty-two' has been carrying, and to a degree forcing, the ideology that veterans commit suicide at an alarming rate. The world is focus fixed on this disturbing number and never focused on the many successes of veterans. They don't cite those who have started companies, or earned degrees and transitioned smoothly on to the next mission. We have become infatuated with the negative and not the positive.

This has created a culture of the most toxic veteran mentality: the thirst for attention, the need for affirmation, and acknowledgement from civilians who didn't join the service. They are the vocal few that make the rest of us look bad. These silly, sad few don't want to do the work. They also don't want to accept that they are the issue. They are the creation of their own calamity. They will never transition when they use transition as a monetary excuse. Until they are ready to embrace the transition and show up to do the work, they keep a steady residence in the rut where they currently exist.

The biggest transition for me so far in my life has been from the military. Getting out was as uncomfortable as showing up to high school for the first time. I experienced the same thought process of wondering, will I fit in? Will I be able to survive? I can say I had more excuses to not make it work, than most. My kids definitely gave me the motivation to stay in the fight. I applied for 15 jobs, my motivation was making sure the kids would not starve. I carry a heavy obligation as a man and provider to do just that, provide. I didn't have the option for excuses at that point.

I remember my first job interview the gentleman asked me, "What is your definition of Leadership?"

Little did he know I had just spent months learning this before going to my Non-Commissioned Officer promotion board.

"Leadership is influencing people by providing purpose, direction, and motivation while operating to accomplish the mission and improving the organization. Purpose gives subordinates the reason to act in order to achieve a desired outcome. Providing clear direction involves communicating how to accomplish a mission: prioritizing tasks, assigning responsibility for completion, and ensuring subordinates understand the standard. Motivation supplies the will to do what is necessary to accomplish a mission."

I felt like the biggest tool in the room. I couldn't even help it. It's what had been driven into my head for the past few months. Then the next question was, "Have you ever been in a stressful situation and how did you handle it?"

Little did he know I was sixty days back from Afghanistan. On our first mission I was having to call upon my big gun to provide cover fire so we could get a casualty to a safe location so a medic could do work. I was fresh out of Regiment and the first thought of my day, everyday, was about the boys. I wanted to know what were they doing and what I was missing. I hated it. I knew my days of running and gunning were over. That did not mean I liked it or truly accepted it.

A phrase I learned from my baseball coach growing up and have held onto ever since is this quote, "If you are living in the past, you are dying in the present."

I wish I could put this into words in a perfectly articulate way, but I will try. We tend to demonize our transition, as if it is harder for us to transition than others. Granted, combat veterans tend to see some ugly stuff. And I won't denigrate anyone's experience knowing I have had plenty of my own. But we can't forget the rest of the people in our world who see death daily, and for longer periods of time. Doctors, nurses, firefighters, and cops see death and gore all the time. My father was a thirty-two year veteran of the Los Angeles City fire department. In his career he has been called to some serious incident scenes, and some of those have definitely remained with him for a long time. The fear of children drowning was one of those triggers for him. Being a father of four and running multiple calls a summer on small children who were lost to the unfortunate death by drowning, still raises his blood pressure. It scares him even now when my kids are visiting and take a swim in his pool.

Once we can acknowledge that we aren't alone in this world of mental and emotional trauma, then we can stop feeling entitled to extra attention and consideration. Yes, combat veterans could use a greater effort from the Department of Defense on debriefing combat stressors. But we can't be so self-indulgent to think we should be the only focus in society getting told, "Thank you for your service."

The hard truth is most PTSD is something that can be treated with proper counseling. So then, now what? What's the next excuse you hear about the struggle of getting out of the military? Jobs? I had a veteran once asking me for money. This actually happens a lot, and my first question in response is to ask if they currently have a job. The answer is almost always, no. This answer offends me. They are fully capable of getting a job. I assume they feel like no one has ever walked in their shoes, but here they stood, looking into the eyes of a man that had been there. Then I ask, why not? There are always a million excuses for why they can't find gainful employment.

I once told a gentleman this, "Please do me a favor. If

you want my help, I need you to do something for me first. Head over to McDonald's and Walmart tomorrow morning. Wear something nice, shave, and put on a tie. Make sure to smell good, and ask if they are hiring. If they are, apply immediately. Then, call me tomorrow and I will help you."

He called me the next day and told me he got the job at Walmart. I had no intention of giving this gentleman money because I didn't have any money to give. But I also told him how I felt about someone who was asking me for help but had not made the effort to first help himself.

How could I be so mean? How dare I be so forward? The simple answer is because I have been in the position many times where I didn't know how I was going to pay my mortgage or how I was going to buy my kids anything for Christmas. You know what I did? I applied for jobs. Driving Uber and being a car salesman were just a couple of my many jobs back then. I was able to work the hard hours at the used car lot during the day, and pick up hours driving Uber in between. I don't think I will ever make assumptions about an Uber driver ever again.

All those things, I did on top of filming the movie, 'Range 15,' and owning a two-million-dollar company. My net worth was about five million-dollars at the time. I had a cool one-hundred dollars in my checking account, and a big fat zero in savings. I didn't blame the VA. I didn't curse the MAN. I wouldn't damn the Holy Spirit. I blamed myself for being terrible with money and making terrible life choices. So it was up to me to find a way to pay my bills. Working multiple jobs was my only answer.

We tend to want to blame everyone else for our bad choices. It is a very human temptation. Until we make the conscious decision to look inward for solutions we will always have that little voice tempting us to place the blame outward. The best wisdom I can give about transition is this: You are not alone. This isn't a veteran issue. This is a humanity issue.

I got out of the military expecting to have transition issues because the community told me it was what inevitably happened. I was expected to hate the VA and have trouble finding a job. I was told that it was going to be hard because people wouldn't understand me. I believe this idea and mindset set me up for failure.

Who the fuck was I to expect the world to care about my life? It's a selfish idea to impose my issues onto the world. It contradicts who I am as a person and undermines my character. My mother raised a hard worker and my father raised a fighter. But I believed my community and consequently I allowed myself to fall victim to a toxic mindset. I was egotistical and cocky about my experiences. I was entitled. I wanted the world to not only care about what I did, but I also wanted them to thank me for my service. I am disgusted as I write this to even admit I allowed myself to be this way. My father would kick me in the ass for acting this way as a child. He didn't bring me up that way.

I had my issues, I felt guilty for not being on a mission where I lost two of the most influential persons in my military career. I was injured in Ranger School and wasn't allowed to deploy on the next rotation. I had taken a bad fall during patrols in the Mountain Phase. I fell down the side of a hill and thankfully my rucksack cushioned and broke my fall. The only negative about that, was my traps took the impact, and my right brachial plexus nerve was damaged, rendering my right arm temporarily useless. This was an injury that took almost a year to heal. Even to this day there is some feeling lost in my scapula area.

When it came time for my unit to deploy, my bags were packed, and I was in the battalion hallway when my NCOIC said I couldn't go. At that moment I had mixed emotions. I wanted to go to war with the boys. I missed them and loved my job. And now that I had my Ranger Tab, I would be in a better position. But having only one arm working, I knew it could pose a problem. It was nice to be home for a while, to enjoy my two kids at the time and try and build my relationship with them. But once I found out about my brothers' passing, I was crushed. I wanted to be there, and I wished it were me. I thought to myself, maybe I could have handled the bullets better than they did. Maybe I would have been able to help them with the minimal medical training I had.

I wished it were me for so long because those men were better men than I could ever be, and I didn't feel worthy of life over them. Do you know what it's like, that I looked up to two men that were younger than me? They had trained some of the best and I imagine would have continued down that path. They could have made an even bigger footprint in the Army than they already had. I would have gladly traded places with them. It is humbling and instills profound vulnerability to know the best have gone down. That puts things into perspective and showed me just how insignificant I was. This carried on for many years. I felt I almost had to drink myself stupid to show them I still cared. I caused pain to myself out of guilt. If I weren't hungover on the day after the anniversary of their deaths, then I wasn't celebrating them properly.

This pattern carried on for years. I found reasons to drink on their behalf. Both men drank Miller Lite while serving, so I felt if I was drinking I would start off by having two Miller Lites for them. I still do this sometimes, but now it's almost a 'tilt of the hat to my boys.' Before it was to acknowledge the thrashing I was about to give my liver, but I was always doing so in 'their memory.' I don't know where this idea came from and why I wasn't alone in this strange ritual. It took me years of this to finally somehow snap out of it. I was holding onto a lot of guilt. I victimized myself and was slowly killing the person I knew I should be. I came to the revelation that there is no way my boys were looking down on me saying, "That's it big guy, get so blitzed you punch holes in the wall; yeah Ranger buddy that's it. Take another shot, that's what makes us proud."

When you step back and think about this idea, it is so fucking foolish. But thousands do this daily. I finally came to the conclusion that maybe, just maybe they were looking down on me saying, "Do something with that fucking life my man, make it worthwhile. Do it for us." I stopped living for their memory and started living for them. I wanted to live the life that they didn't get to finish living.

My new transition wasn't going to make me forget my friends. It wasn't going to result in their honorable service being lost and forgotten, or that their sacrifices were in vain. My new transition meant I was going to do them proud. I wasn't going to feed my self-indulgent pity anymore over our loss of them. Stopping the excuses and the twisted thinking were my keys to a new freedom to pursue my own dreams. And now I'm living them, with a greater sense of pride in myself, knowing they would be giving me the biggest high-five of all my friends.

I spent some years in the Border Patrol once I left the

Army. Living the life SSG Barraza said he wanted when he finished his time. In 2004 on my first deployment I was already planning on what I was going to do once I got out. He would laugh because I was barely in the military and I was already planning my escape.

I remembered my father used to come home from work smelling like a house fire. I thought it would be cool to combine my Airborne skills with firefighting and become a Smoke Jumper. At least, that was one of my ideas for my post military career. But SSG Barraza explained to me that the Border Patrol had a special operations team and solid funding for training. He said it would be the closest thing to being a Ranger in the civilian world. I was living his dream for him. At the time I was happy, but still a part of me was missing. I was still having these depression pity parties from time to time. The 'shoulda- coulda- woulda's' that were making me feel like I couldn't be content in this life were dragging me down. How can I be happy living someone else's dream? Why haven't I started living my own dream?

But what was that dream, what was my path? I needed badly to find it and stop fighting the inevitable. I was so tired of fighting all the time. I don't mean tired, as in, I couldn't continue. I was just tired of fighting with no real purpose or direction that would take me anywhere better. I was just fighting change because I still believed I needed to struggle with this transition. I was wrong and naive to believe that. And I wish every transitioning veteran knew that before they engaged in their struggles.

Fighting it will not get you anywhere, while rising for it will take you everywhere. I know this from my years of resisting simple things as change and transition; you can't just wish for it, you need to also work for it. And the sad reality is that you don't get to see the actual hard work I put in to these endeavors. You just see the results. Maybe someone has caught a glimpse of me in my dress greens. Or, they caught sight of some of the decorations that were pinned to my chest. Maybe it was seeing a few funny jokes in a YouTube video, or catching the guy playing a motorcycle club member on TV, those are what everyone sees and admires. The hard work doesn't even make the 'B' roll. I sometimes wish it would make it, though.

It was time I turned the page in my transition. In the reference that was taught to me, turning the page was meant to direct you to forget the mistake that was made on the field, and get set to just play the rest of the game. It's a long game and if you allow one mistake take over your mind, you will continue to fuck up on all the other plays. It is consistently a downward spiral from there. Once this train is in motion, there is no stopping it. If it gets away completely, only death, destruction, and mayhem lie in its path. And that isn't just a metaphor for baseball, it's applicable to all things in life.

We don't need to fear the transition because people have told us to fear it at every turn. We need to show up and log the hours. Do the work and don't quit. Stop listening to the negative voices that influence your thinking and convincing you that transition is terrible, scary, or impossible to overcome. We are our only obstacles. And making up your mind to not let transition own you, is the most important mental transition you will ever make. Why would you wait? Knowing now it can't beat you or own you, why give it another day? Why even give it another second? Start now with that mental transition to owning your life in your new world. We don't have to believe something just because that something is told to us by someone we admire or respect. And I appreciate the irony here, that you're reading these words in MY self help book.

But that is almost exactly my point. You should absolutely question things that make you feel negative. Because when someone is trying to rent space in your head with their words, don't you think they should at least do you the courtesy of making it positive and productive for your life? Shouldn't the people you love and respect most in life be encouraging you to grow and change into the best human being you are capable of being? Wouldn't it be great if growth and change were phases of life that were celebrated by the military and the civilian world, all in concert to support our fellow man? Maybe we should all endeavor to be better about it.

In fact, I will take it one step further and say we should all just do this as a habit anyway. When you have a friend, no matter who you are, that is seeming like they need a change but fear the transition, give them encouragement. Push them to grow within themselves so they can realize their potential. Give them the high five, pat on the ass, or smack upside the head that tells them not only that they CAN do it, but that they NEED to do it.

Transition shouldn't be feared, no matter who you are, or where you are in life. Transitions are as common as breathing and birthdays, so we should focus on living and eating cake sometimes. Be there for your friends as a force of good to change the conversation about transition. Do as Ghandi said and be the change you want to see in the world. You really can't go wrong with that.

Chapter Three

The Asshole In Mirror - Self Accountability

Everyday I have to wake up and reinvent my mind, like spent brass on the tile. Taking the burden of a lost soul and letting it fall to the floor...

because these shoulders are tired and I can't bear the weight anymore.

I know it's not my problem truth be told, but if you understood these boots I was expected to fill you would know the pressure I hold.

I didn't just carry that casket and that was the end, I have held that weight in my heart again and again. I can't just go peacefully in this night. Have too much tied into this life.

My heart has been torn in so many directions, not sure what the truth is anymore in my reflection.

Is it sad when you can't recognize yourself? Look at your face and all you see is someone else?

I have lived a majority of my days, thinking... was I always supposed to end this way?

Was I always going to be in this pain? Was I supposed to teeter on the sane and insane?

Held the guilt for so many years, why was it I that had to see his family in tears?

Handing them the gold star with grief. They look at me like their child's accomplice.... soul thief.

Now we battle with conflicts of self and where we stand. We are losing ourselves by our own hand.

That hand that feeds the magazine, the hand that holds the weapon... Which shoots the enemy.

Hands and fingers made to touch and feel, but instead turned on ourselves for our own lives to steal.

Stop reaching for that escape. You should be reaching for that open door of community. You should be letting your brothers in, and asking for immunity.

You see every time I see another person who decided to take the wrong door... it's another battle lost in the big picture of war.

We fought, but now we continue to fight for life. We fight out of love of each other, for love of ourselves and significant other.

I have cried myself to sleep when no one is looking... I am man enough to say, I need help and I am not joking.

I lost myself, and everything that was me.

So I became alone... caged in a savage world, I became angry.

I have been there... in a hole so dark no night vision or flash could help me find my path.

I have burned myself alive, from the inside out... alcohol, painkillers, numbing self doubt. I submit the prescriptions I know I don't need... but if the Doctor says so, who am I to disbelieve?

It's like I'm two people, Dr. Jekyll and Mr. Hyde... what you see during daylight, isn't the man I am at night.

Slurs of an alcohol fueled slumber. I can still feel it creeping in a blink of an eye...

When I turn to my friends, I have lost count, and lost hope. Funny thing is they are in the same boat. We say cheers to the fallen, for sacrifice made... we all know the price, we know what's been paid.

We are in the same place, we lost a piece of our puzzle. Still trying to get it, find it... forever in struggle.

Sometimes I feel I'm pulled in two separate directions... one minute firmly on feet, and the next in depression.

I am always two steps from destroying the core... I feel some nights, the best part of me was lost in war.

Would they be acting the way that I am? Living with life, so ready to give in. I can't believe they would take this so lightly. This fight is not over, it's daily and nightly.

Being light infantry wasn't just an MOS anymore... My first battle is getting my feet on the floor.

Quick to the painkillers, just to gather my vision... will I make it through today, will I survive this mission?

What made me this way? What caused this corruption? I was such a peaceful child growing up. Now I am struggling just not to self destruct.

Don't think I haven't been there before... in the dark and alone..looking for that exit door.

I can't tell you why I didn't choose that chance. My destiny simply isn't ready to be done with this dance.

But when it's dark as night and I can't see the light. I remember... this is my book, and I'll continue to fight. The last chapter in this life, it's mine to write...

Sometimes I feel I'm already halfway in the afterlife, so I call on those that have walked the same roads, dealt with the same fight.

Those exposed to what most could never understand...

the trials of war, the trials of man. We stand together to conquer the fear. To soldier the weather, ... can the weather stop a soldier that's come back from days that were colder than anyone has ever seen?

I had to intervene, because I awoke from a dream... one of you struggling with the demons of war.

I know what you feel, I've been there before...

I know you have my back, and I have yours.

When I wrote this, I wanted to find a way to talk about the struggles of transition but do it in a way no one else has done yet. Spoken word has always inspired me. Something about the delivery of a poem in physical form has always intrigued me. In this poem I wanted to artistically express all my personal struggles and journey after getting out. I was finally getting my life back together after a divorce, and felt I didn't want to forget what it took to get back on my feet. Maybe I would be able to show others that they aren't alone. We are all going though it, and just that idea, in and of itself, is empowering.

You are not alone.

I get so sick of people waiting on the world to create a path. I'm just an average dude with extraordinary drive and a lack of respect toward following the rules. When the world said, "Here is how it's done," I told the world, "I will find another way." They tell you there are concrete ways of making it in this life. I have found that to be completely false. There isn't a true single direction or method to living. It's just a destination with imagination. Find a goal. Create that path. You are the keeper of your destiny.

My mother came from humble beginnings. And I mean humble beginnings, living with eight siblings and two adults in a two room house. It was a kind of poverty that most Americans have never seen and will never experience.

She was just one of those people who didn't feel sorry for her situation, but made the best of it. This incredible woman I call my mother was born in a suburb of El Paso, Texas. She was the second born in her family. Her mother was born in Mexico and her father was a first generation American. Her father and grandfather both served in the military. They were just hard working Americans doing their thing, just making enough money to make ends meet.

My mom grew up working at a very young age. When she was around eight years old, her grandfather took her to work in the fields, picking cotton. Just to put it in perspective, she would work to try to buy herself a pair of shoes. She worked hours in the fields to earn enough money to afford a pair of shoes, even if it was just a used pair. My mother remembers the days of growing up and working her summers in the onion fields. By the time she turned eleven, she was responsible for taking care of her four siblings. She would go to school, and if the family needed more money, she would go work more hours on other odd jobs such as pouring milk for the Dairy farm into bottles, to eventually becoming a waitress. On school days she would return home to help with her siblings while her mother cooked dinner, cleaned the house, and did the laundry. After school it was also my mom's responsibility to iron the clothes for the entire family. She never had any brand-new toys for Christmas. Her biggest dream was to get a new doll. What she ended up getting was one used doll with some hair missing, for one Christmas. It was one of the greatest Christmases she remembers, and the happiest one she had because the doll was new to her.

As she grew, she knew she wanted more out of life. I point this out because I always question where I get my drive. My mom, she wanted more, and I get my relentless drive from her.

She decided she didn't want to be the same person who lived in the same little town. It was small town called Canutillo, just outside of El Paso, Texas where she took control of her life. She wanted more than the status quo of working in the cannery or in a factory for the rest of her life. Even if it meant living in a tiny little shack if she could afford it, or a trailer if she could afford that, she was determined to change her path. She intended on living any life other than what she had growing up, in an adobe house. She wanted more than that. So, she put it in her head that she wanted to go to LA. Los Angeles, California is the City of Angels. It seemed, and still now seems, to be where everyone goes to seek out and realize their dreams of being an actor or actress. It is the city where people go to live life a little bit more. She had it in her heart to grow to be more than what she was.

Her decision made, she packed her few belongings.

She had a toothbrush, toothpaste, a hairbrush, a single change of clothes, and nothing more. Everything she owned could fit into a brown grocery bag. Take that in for a moment. Consider your life and imagine what it would look like if everything you owned could fit into a bag that would normally hold your groceries.

She bought a ticket and got on a bus. She didn't cower to fear, though I'm sure she had some. Just like that she boarded a Greyhound bus to Los Angeles, California. She started there.

Her first job was a gas attendant, but she kept her hours and was dedicated in her work. She didn't fear any type of hard work because there was little any city based job could throw at her that she couldn't handle. My mom went straight to the belly of every beast or task. She knew she was capable of doing the hard work.

She just kept getting better jobs, one step at a time. Growing and growing was the result of her unwavering strength of character and commitment to have a better future than her past.

My father grew up in the streets, he was the stereotypical street kid. His father was a hard man, and abusive to the whole family. The main target of his abuse was always my grandmother. He was a drinker, and when he drank, he had a heavy hand. That's why my father spent a lot of time on the streets with his brother. He took the escape of being outside his father's sight, and consequently his reach.

My father always carried those invisible scars with him. By nature, he was a fighter and he spent a lot of time out running around. He learned about gangs by watching what he saw from the gangs that lived and ran in his neighborhood. The warlords would have these crazy fights. Once, he told me a story about watching a couple guys fight with a belt. It was significant to him. In that fight, he saw the power. He witnessed the camaraderie they had. He was seeing the family life that he wished for, thirsted for, but never actually had. By the time he was thirteen, his mother did her best to get away from the abusive relationship with his father and she ran off to Los Angeles, California with her kids. And that's where he stayed, growing up in the streets of Echo Park. By the age of fourteen he was jumped into the Echo Park street gang. It was his new family and the street he protected.

When he was sixteen years old, he and his buddy were going to another part of the neighborhood to go see a girl. That typical 'girl that lives in the wrong neighborhood, but you want to see her.' They got jumped. My father carried with him a small pipe when he was younger for protection. He hit a guy with it and subsequently got arrested. The probation officer gave him an option to go to jail or join the military.

My father joined the United States Marine Corps. After several years of service he met my mom and she kept him on the right path. He had always wanted to enjoy the family lifestyle. This foreign lifestyle that looked so great on TV shows he watched, but had never actually experienced, was what he ultimately wanted. He didn't have the structure of a father to keep him in line. He didn't have a strong example of how to lead a family and be their provider and protector. He didn't have the luxury of a mother telling him what to do because she was always consumed with worrying about the rest of the kids. Left on his own, he's always done his own thing. But never has he ever shown us that he shirks his responsibilities or doesn't take full accountability for all his actions.

I say all this just to explain where I'm coming from. That is, I am from a family who has gone through a tough life and had a lot of life experiences. I've always questioned myself. What does that mean? What makes me tick? What drives me to be who I am today? The answer always comes back the same for each question. It all leads back to my mom. My mom and my dad both showed me the way; but primarily it was my mom. To know that my Mother was picking cotton around the age of eight years old so she can help buy the necessities and help her parents, is one of the most humbling things I've ever learned. One of the most basic human needs of a family was met by my mother when she was just a child. As a young girl and even after leaving her home, my mom and a few of her siblings, felt obligated to continue to contribute to the family to lessen the financial burden and worked tirelessly.

For me to understand where she started and where she ended up, I never wanted to disrespect the idea of what she's done. I needed to appreciate the hard work she has relentlessly put toward giving herself a better life. If I for some reason didn't advance from where she left off, I feel I would not be doing her life full of sacrifice, any justice. And I would not feel that I'm offering proper respect for the example she has given to me.

And so, with tremendous respect and deference to my pillar of a mother, I continue to drive. I've never witnessed her even in a moment of weakness not take full accountability for her life and all the circumstances surrounding it. She meets every task ready to do everything it takes. It isn't because she has some crazy physical ability. It's because she lays blame on no one but herself and has an indomitable spirit. She is a warrior, and raised me to be a warrior, too. It's because of this I take responsibility for my victories and failures in the same way. Everything is my fault, life is so much simpler that way. It also means I can change whatever I need to change in order to make it better.

I continue to push and push harder all the time to be the most successful person I can be. Hopefully now, she can watch me grow and succeed. I want her to continue seeing the success that I have is one-hundred percent based on the drive that she handed me. It is due to the fact that I want to give her all the respect she so rightfully deserves for what she's done to help us get to the position that we are in as a family, today. She is the foundation of our family and our rock. She is that glue that holds us all together. Never once did she blame her parents or anyone else for not having a lot growing up, because she knew her parents did the best they could. She felt that leaving her home was the only way to better herself and her life, and to continue to help them. She was successful in many ways. Leading and protecting our family through every adversity and never faltering, she was successful.

One lonely night, I believe it was when I was in Kentucky, the strangest thing happened to me. I'm not sure how it happened, but for some reason this crazy thing came to pass one night when I was sitting in my little apartment.

That building was actually a brothel years before I moved in. It was long before I lived there of course. But I know this because one of the days I was getting dropped off while working as a bouncer, my buddy told me.

"Hey! This place is where my dad had his bachelor party, back in the day before he and my mom got married."

I was surprised and doubtful, "You kiddin' me?"

"Yeah, yeah... this used to be a well-known brothel."

So now I'm living in an old brothel that only costs two-hundred dollars per month for everything. I'm talking all utilities- electric, water, garbage -everything was included for just two-hundred dollars per month. I was just working as a waiter and bouncer. But as I was sitting there I realized, I could change my life dramatically, in one day. In one day, I can make the decision to change everything. And I also knew that in the making of that change, I would have to face some sacrifice. And that sacrifice might have to be being broke. That sacrifice might be going into debt. That sacrifice might even mean losing my life in combat.

The next day I woke up, took a shower and went straight to the recruiter. I decided then and there to make a change. I decided I wanted to change my life. I decided to do something drastic, something out of the ordinary. I needed this change.

What I was doing was working as a waiter, working as a bouncer, spending my money to get drunk, and doing it all again on one big repeat cycle. It was a vicious cycle that I realized was not going to put me in the position I wanted to be in to secure my future. I wasn't taking the right steps.

I was too busy complaining about not being academically eligible for school. I was too busy being mad for being cut from several independent professional baseball teams that I had tried out for. I was angry at the world because life was not going my way. And the truth of the matter was not only simple, but it was right in front of me. I wasn't making the right decisions.

I stopped pointing my finger at other people and started looking in the mirror. I faced myself and decided to change my life that day. Once I went to the Army recruiter, I knew that I signed up to change my life. I have continued to do things like this for the rest of my life to date. I made decisions that might not have been the most popular. Some of my choices have not been the easiest, but I made them based on the outright desire to change my life.

The simple act of looking myself in the mirror and saying to that old me, "I need to change my life, I want to change my life," has led me out of some dark places and away from a path that wouldn't lead me to better myself.

If I'm stuck in a rut or there is something going wrong in my life, and I'm not happy with it, I fucking change it. I don't care how much fucking shit people talk to me about.

I don't care how much my parents say, "it looks like you're unstable."

I don't care how much of anything happens around

that change, because the whole idea behind it is to adjust and straighten out my life. I'm the one who knows what's good and bad for my life. The buck stops with me, because I'm my own personal expert. Generally speaking, I'm the reason why my life doesn't go well. Actually, I am one-hundred percent of the reason. When my life is going to shit, I have to sit back and reevaluate who I am, what I'm doing, and why I'm doing it. Then I need to decide whether I want to continue to do this thing that is steering me wrong. And if I continue doing it anyway, I'm doing so knowing that my life is not going to be in a place where I'm happy. That's the FACTS, man.

The fact is I have to fucking make these choices. But if I don't have the fucking intestinal fortitude to look at myself and evaluate the things I'm doing and choices I'm making, with the most brutal honesty I can summon, then I can't fucking come out with a self-bettering mindset or anything that can benefit me. If I can look at myself and say, "Alright, bud, you're doing pretty good," – then I'm moving in the right direction.

Until I can admit I have a fucking problem, I can't start fixing that problem. It's the same rule they give people in twelve-step programs, or AA meetings, you have to first accept the fact that you have a problem. Then from there you have the ability to start working on, and hopefully fixing, that problem. And that's exactly what it is for veterans all over the world. And it is not even just veterans, it applies to people in general. You have to recognize the fact that you've been blaming everyone else instead of yourself. The good news is that once you start blaming yourself and assuming the responsibility you can move in a positive direction. Once you start seeing that you have to make those steps and that you have to do the work, you will have the ability to overcome the reasons your life is so fucked up right now. There is so much power in just that one little thing, admitting that there is a problem, and YOU can fix it.

Once you accept and truly BELIEVE that, you can begin the changes needed to improve your life. But you have to accept that the reason you are in the position you are today is because of the things you have done, yourself. When you FUCKING ACCEPT THAT, DEEP IN YOUR FUCKING HEART- now you're ready to make a change. Now you can initiate self rescue, because you've identified that you are the threat. Right? You've identified that you're the asshole in the mirror that keeps fucking up your life. You now have the decision before you to alter your course and head in the right direction. And once you've done that you can start taking the steps to get it done.

Really quickly, do a self evaluation and ask yourself how much of your time and effort you are investing in doing these things:

(1) your vice of choice,

(2) fitness,

(3) and drinking.

Your vice may be video games, fast food, recreational drugs, sex, partying, or social media. It is any other thing that takes time away from the productive things in life.

vice:(as defined by Merriam-Webster) - an immoral or evil habit or practice.

Think about that definition for a minute. EVIL. That's a strong word, evil. But it gets right to the heart of the description of a vice, doesn't it? Anything taking your effort, time, and money away from living at your best and having a good life, really is evil.

These things must all be brought under control in order to keep you on your path to betterment. Reign it all in. Every bad thing trying to distract you from self-betterment and a good life, round it up and scrutinize it like hell.

Drinking is probably a majority and source of most people's issues, but we know there are others, like I listed above. These are the things I'm talking about. You can change your life in one day. By simply changing your mind and taking initiative to do what needs doing, your life can move in a better direction.

You need a day of reflection. You need a day to examine every aspect of your life and admit that you are fucked up. After taking that day of acknowledging that you're the one fucking up your life, you will have enabled yourself to start taking the steps necessary to fix it.

That is so fucking honest, and as real as I can be. People come to me and often say things like, "Look, man! I want to be like you, Rocco. I want to fucking do acting, man. I want to be a funny guy, man. I want to be like that! I want to be on TV."

My answer to these guys is always, "Are you sure?"

Are you sure you really want to do this for a living? Before you commit to it, have to educated yourself on this path? Is it something that looks fun? Is it something that you are ready for? You will feel alone, you will feel defeated more often than not. And that moment when you feel you have made some progress, more doors will close. Are you sure you have thought this through? You have to remember your motivation practically every minute, because that moment you forget why you are doing it, that second you doubt yourself- someone else is filling that position. You need to know this road isn't easy and no matter what, no matter how- you will have to find the drive to push through.

That's what it takes to make it in this business; someone that has to want it more than the voice in their own head doubting them.

This is true for any job or career that you look at and admire, thinking you would love to have it. Every job that is visible to the masses, most likely took a lot of hard work, dedication, and sacrifice. You can have one of those awesome jobs too! Just be ready to change your mindset to be ready and willing to do all the work to get it. So if that's really what you want, get started on doing the work to your own path to happiness and self-betterment.

George Bernard Shaw may have been seen as a bit of an oddball in his time, but he had some wisdom when it came to accountability. He once said, "Progress is impossible without change, and those who cannot change their minds cannot change anything." That is some true shit right there. Even back over a hundred years ago, he was talking about changing your life by changing your mind. There has to be something to that, right? Because here and now, a century later, we are still managing to fuck it up and having to discuss it in the written and spoken word. Get yourself the life you deserve by deciding to change your mind and make the steps you need to have it. Take the first step to own your shit and hold yourself accountable for all the things you need to do. Focus on the lesson, not the mistake.

We don't learn by not making any mistakes. We learn by making them and owning them. We accumulate wisdom and experience by focusing on what we can learn from each of those mistakes and trying not to make them again. If we focus on our past, we will be stuck there. If we own our past, and take all we've learned, we can grow into a better future. Nobody escaped the future by running from their past. It just doesn't work that way. So don't be afraid to take accountability for yourself and your actions and make them better.

Chapter Four

Who The Fuck Am I? - Identity

THE 5 STAGES OF THE VETERAN TRANSITION EVOLUTION

(Not all veterans go through all of these, but I'm willing to bet many have taken a similar path to some extent or another.)

1. Veteran with entitlement

This is the one who is always looking for a handout, looking for the government to help them because it's what is owed to them for serving their country. This is the one who forgets that his service to the country was a volunteer decision, and nobody owes him anything.

Note: A lot of veterans have trouble finding jobs. If I went to apply for a job at McDonald's today I would get that job. Do I feel I deserve more? Of course, but if I need to eat and feed my family I will start at any job and build myself up one step at a time. I know this because I've done it. This isn't about not getting the benefits owed to you. Get them and use them. Just don't get out and expect the world to magically hand you a career.

2. Veteran with self-pity

This is a tough one, a lot of us lost friends in some way. This is the one who holds on to the anniversary dates for a reason to get trashed, and feels bad because he is still living. He suffers a severe case of survivor's guilt- the shoulda, coulda, wouldas. He is the one who doesn't realize he is wasting the very life his friend would have done anything for one more day of. He does not realize how little respect he is actually showing his friend by wasting his life mired in guilt and pity. It's time to grow, time to move forward; if not for you, for them.

Note: I still struggle with this from time to time, I can find a reason to drink any day of the week because it reminds me of them. But this is a downward spiral, and I have to step back and regroup. I know in my consciousness I cannot live my life in such a way. I resolved long ago to make them proud in a real and productive way by doing right in my life.

3. Veteran with identity issues

This one holds on to the military years as if they are what

define him. He holds on to being Infantry as if anyone in the civilian world really cares. These are the 'Al Bundys' of the veteran world – they scored four touchdowns in one game back in the day, but are now miserable shoe salesmen. They hold on to what they did and don't realize it honestly means nothing if you aren't doing anything now.

Note: Be proud of what you have done, but understand it won't carry you in the civilian world. You have to take the skills learned in the military and apply them to your new world.

4. Veteran who feels like being a veteran makes them better than the rest of society

This veterans feels that because they served, it makes them better than the person who didn't. They think they are better and deserve more. They don't realize the civilian world also deals with PTSD, loss, and depression, and that civilians also have transitions in life and fall on hard times. We are all human and we all have our own stuff, but most people don't look down on others for that. They find peace and continue moving forward, building lifelong bonds with people who care and can relate. They live knowing we all have our issues and we all find ways of getting through them.

Note: Before you were in the military you were a civilian. Only three-percent of Americans have served, which means most employers won't know – or care – what you have been through. They just want to hire quality workers.

5. The veteran who gets through these stages to realize he is a civilian now, a civilian who has a set of tools he learned in the military; and that these tools can make him successful.

Note: The world has been so focused on the negative side of the veteran transition; I wanted to put together a very blunt and uncomfortable view on the different personalities of veterans transitioning. I want to look at the toxic mindsets. To be brutally honest in this community can get you excommunicated by the masses that might not agree. The fact is, it's hard to be mad at these statements when they are so close to the truth. Transitioning is similar to mourning a death, a death of a military career essentially and moving on to new life. This is the mental path I took, it was a long road. Here is the reality, I have made my way through all these and have now found peace within myself. This isn't meant to be a negative post but rather a post of self-reflection.

Who the Fuck Am I? Learning and accepting your identity. How do you learn who you are? It's pretty simple, really. You go out and DO shit. You try new things. You take some risks. Push outside your warm little comfort zone of mediocre. You will never know you aren't supposed to be a bartender, doctor, or mountain climber until you go out and try those things. For me, I learned the tough lesson that I wasn't a firefighter. It took me a year to figure that shit out. I was fighting a fire on a burning bus. With raging flames causing havoc all around me, I was the lead man on the hose. I was exactly where I had worked so hard to be. And you know what I thought?

"This isn't me, this isn't where I want to be in life."

How does a person just become okay with who they are? Is it really even possible to become okay with who you are? The problem is that we have too many people wanting to be something they naturally are not. For example, I don't know what it's like to just be born cool. Some people are just born cool, right? They have to be. There is no physical way that some of the cool people I have met in my life were not just born that way. Coming out of the womb wearing a leather jacket, smiling at the right times, and saying all the smoothest things. Some guys are just born cool.

On the other side of that, some people are born awkward. That's all fucking good and dandy because I think awkward happens a lot more often than cool. The problems occur when one of these tries to fit in and be opposite of what they were born. It's the person who was born cool and tries to be awkward, or the person who is awkward tries to be cool, it just doesn't fucking work. You can easily tell there is some dishonesty in their character. When you speak and interact with them, it never quite feels like you are seeing the real person. It is as if you can feel the fake.

It is people that are honestly good with who they are that draw attention and possess natural attraction. People that live in their skin comfortably and are truly good with who they are at their core? These rare people have accepted they are inherently, one way or the other, and are completely at peace with that characteristic. It is because they are honest with themselves and how they show their true character to the world. There is nothing to hide once they know who they are. There is nothing more and nothing less, they don't put on any kind of pretense. It is as if they silently announce to the world, "here is who I am."

I really do give it my sincere effort in my everyday life to be completely honest. Within that daily effort, I really focus on not lying to myself. I know it sounds like a circular argument, but that's how I break it down. Putting these practices into short and simple methods is the way it makes sense to me. The simple idea of not lying to myself has become another way I can better myself. I am able to look at myself objectively, and get the truth easily. Then I am able to find a solution for what might need help. I know I'm overweight. I know I have a bad receding hairline. I get it. I accept it. And then, I don't give a fuck. Why not? Because this is me. And when you're able to get to that point in your existence, being good with who you are, you are freed from having the insecurities that slow most people down. A man that knows who he is and fully accepts it, is a man in control of his own destiny. Or at least he is on his way to being there.

I think insecurities are the craziest things. What completely blows my mind is the way people try so hard to fight and conceal those insecurities from the rest of the world. But what the people that hide their insecurities don't realize, is that they bleed out into their everyday behaviors.

When men are insecure about other men, or women are insecure about other women, it ends up coming out and showing itself in their interactions. When friends are insecure with each other, or brothers and sisters are insecure with each other, jealousies tend to form. Eventually, as I'm sure everyone reading this has seen, those insecurities and the actions based on them, will destroy any of those relationships.

These dangerous, toxic feelings begin to take on a life of their own, becoming something that is just ugly, and it doesn't need to live in the space of your mind. I like to ask myself, 'Why am I allowing anyone to have that kind of power over me?' Someone that makes me feel insecure means they have power over me. And they only have that power because I'm allowing it. So for that time I let those negative feelings live in my mind, they own me. Someone else is owning my emotions in that case, and I'm never going to be okay with that.

That whole idea to me is fucking bullshit, to allow someone to own and control my emotions. For someone to get me upset, means they have controlled me. This is true whether it is in the biggest or the smallest sense of your being.

I want to be in total control of myself at all times, especially in terms of my mind and emotions. That includes being coherent about exactly what I am feeling and completely understanding of my self-worth, my self-value, and just plain self-respect. It goes along with my sense of self-esteem. And it has a lot to do with being true to oneself. We all know there are a lot of people out there that are fake. Being fake or hiding who you really are doesn't help you grow or live happily. It will never serve you in the sense of trying to accomplish your goals. You can't figure out who you are when you're playing the role of someone else. So just stick to the script you were born with since it will be the most natural for you.

Digging deep inside oneself to figure out what makes them tick is going to take some work. What makes you move? What is your reason for living? Finding out those things, that is the challenge. We all live through years of following social norms and niceties because that's what we are taught to do. Living for one thing, and never really identifying if it was a choice made for the masses, or for yourself, isn't really living. It's just existing.

The best example of this is an eighteen-year-old kid joining the military. At eighteen years old, very few young people know who they are mentally, emotionally, and even physically. Joining the military will inevitably help them find a sense of identity. The problem arises once they are out of the military and that identity is then a minority. It doesn't seem to have a comfortable place existing in civilian culture. They no longer have anyone telling us what to wear, what time to show up, and what the plan was for the next day. It is now completely on them to figure out who they are when no one else is in the room to influence or direct them. This can be a scary space to exist, especially when they are unprepared.

Now you are alone in thought. Wondering perhaps, who am I, and what makes me feel like myself? An uncomfortable truth is that you may be thinking, I have wasted four years of my life and now I am starting back at zero. It's not good to lack direction. Having direction is a basic life necessity. Usually that direction is all based on personal goals. Personal goals are based on your mission, and the mission is based on who you are. So go on and ask yourself, what's your identity?

You cannot find out what you are capable of achieving if you do not first know who, and what, you are. You cannot play to your strengths if you don't know where your weaknesses lie. Again, we revisit that concept of self-reflection.

I took in a deep breath, and as I exhaled, memories of the good old days flooded my mind. A time where I was on the mound, getting ready to close out the game for my team. The crowd was cheering, the lights were bright, the field was chilly, and I was on top of the world. I'm transported back to a time before transitioning out of the military, before there was even a thought to enlist. I was developing my resiliency for a future of being an Army Ranger, there on that mound, that night.

Every veteran deals with life after service a little differently. Some do it well, some self-destruct, and some just muddle along in a kind of post-military no-man's-land. One of the most important things we can do as a country is to help those who have served our nation, get on with their lives after they leave combat behind and once again take up the mantle of private citizenship. This time can be scary and confusing, especially for those young people who haven't yet figured out who they are.

Life is hard for all of us, both in and out of the military. I have lost friends as a kid to gang violence. I have had a significant other attempt suicide right in front of me. I have traveled overseas three times. I have had close friends die in combat and in training. I have been through two divorces, several custody battles, deaths in the family, and teetered on the verge of bankruptcy. As you can see, I have run the gauntlet of life and I am sure there will be more to come. But I adapted and I overcame, so can you. We all just need to work together. We need to help each other understand who we are, and the importance of our places in this big, beautiful world.

Helping veterans adapt to life after service is a challenge I take personally. I have spent the better part of the past three years trying to find ways to help veterans transition out of the military and get on with their lives as smoothly as possible. I know who I am now, and more importantly, I know who I want to be. Helping be part of the solution to helping this generation of veterans make a more smooth and successful transition to civilian life is very important to me as one of those who struggled so hard getting through it.

Like many of my fellow veterans, I have personally had

my share of mishaps in my path to finding normalcy in my life after the military. One of the biggest struggles I had, and have frequently mentioned in my dealings with fellow vets, is dealing with my sense of identity after the military.

Fortunately there are some great veteran-focused non-profits out there, and I have worked with several of them in recent years. There are many out there, but I will only vouch for those from which I have personally seen results.

I have already introduced everyone to a passion of mine, something I loved as a child and that served me well both during my time as an Army Ranger and in my life after.

One of the fondest memories I have of my time after the Army was the time I was able to revisit playing baseball.

"Baseball gives every American boy a chance to excel, not just to be as good as someone else but to be better than someone else. This is the nature of man and the name of the game."- Ted Williams

I experienced a moment of reflection when Heroes Sports gave me the opportunity to get back on that mound and I saw a timeline of my life. It ran from the moment baseball was taken from me for being academically ineligible (no one's fault but my own) to enlisting in the military, and eventually to my life now.

Remember, I started playing baseball when I was only four years old. I had no choice. My father made sure I was playing year-round to keep me out of trouble and away from gangs and street kid mischief. He didn't care if I was the best or the worst. He only cared that I gave one-hundred percent at all times.

It wasn't until years later, standing on that foundation of grit and character, that I finally discovered a true love for the game and elevated myself to a level of success. But reaching that level would have never been possible without those early years of forced participation by the old man. Though I didn't understand it at the time, it remains to this day one of his greatest gifts to me.

For me, baseball is life. For most, baseball is considered boring or monotonous. Baseball the sport is just a sport. I got it. But I see baseball as a whole, very similar to the grind of life. It's a game of failure, a game of negativity. It's a problem to be solved and an obstacle to overcome, just like life itself.

"I had to fight all my life to survive. They were all against me. But I beat the bastards and left them in the ditch."- Ted Williams

Hitting a baseball is considered by some to be the most difficult skill to execute in all sports. Hitting a round ball with a round bat, making contact square-on to get it just right, it's a wicked problem. Sound familiar? Life is nothing but trying to hit one out of the park no matter what field it's pertaining to. Be that relationships, fitness, raising kids, transitioning out of the military, it's all a difficult game. It's just difficult no matter how you cut it. But that doesn't mean it's impossible.

"Every strike brings me closer to the next home run." – Babe Ruth

It is said that baseball is a game of failure, because even the great hitters are only successful thirty-percent of the time. The best pitcher might throw one no-hitter in his entire career. And even the most talented fielder is at the mercy of the batter in terms of whether or not he ever gets the chance to make a play. Typically a score of thirty-percent on any test is well below failure. If I were faithful to my significant other thirty-percent of the time, I wouldn't be in a relationship. If I only paid thirty-percent of my bills, I would be filing for bankruptcy. Nevertheless, life is a game of failure.

We have so many things holding us down. Stress, collapsing relationships, impossible dreams, and unattainable goals are just a few. But like all sports and most of life, it is a game of preparation meeting opportunity.

You have to shake off those unsuccessful moments and keep walking back up to the plate for another chance to knock that ball out of the park. Because the only real truth is, nobody hits a home-run while crying in the dugout. I was a terrible baseball player when I started. But at some point I fell in love with the game. I didn't need anyone to push me after a certain point. I pushed myself. Every day I was outside swinging the bat and soon I was seeing the results on the field. I figured out who I really was. And eventually I figured out who I wanted to be through all these failures.

Don't avoid or run from failures. They can be instrumental in helping you learn your own identity. Those failures and how you rise from them will determine who you are and what you're made of in life. Let them happen and rise up. It doesn't matter how many times you get knocked down, it's the number of times you get back up that really matters. Your determination in getting back up after you fall will say a lot about who you really are as a person. It will also tell the world how badly you want to be successful at all the things you want. Be who you are, and always get back up.

Chapter Five

Motivation - Direction

Why... And Why Me? - By Vincent Vargas

Why?

It's a question people ask me all the time.

Why do I show my family on social media?

Why do I have my life on full display for the world to see?

I try not to boast or gloat; I just show what I got going on. Not some over-processed picture. (Well, other than the ones with the Great One: The Rock.)

Why do I write about my kids?

Why do I write about trying to be a good person?

One of my quotes I often put on Instagram is just: "Be a good dude."

But why do I feel like it's my place to give anyone my opinion?

Here's your answer: I'm using my voice for good and not evil.

I say that to keep things simple... but what I really mean is I am using my voice to show positivity, progress, enjoying the process of life, and to never quit.

In a world consumed with negative news and all the misconceptions of what people want to believe- prejudices, racism, political agendas...

...I'm using my voice for good.

There is so much negative shit. They have the right to post their crap, and I have the right to counter it with my positive content.

I don't need to preach my belief systems. I don't NEED to get anyone to follow me.

But while you are following me, you know what you're going to get....

I want the power of positivity and the Law of Attraction to take hold.

I don't need you to think I'm a good dad. I think my kids are fucking awesome and I post pictures of them whether it's a good day or bad day. That's real.

I don't need to show you how amazing my relationship is. Because to be honest we have good days and frustrating days, but we get along very, very well and that's rare. That's why I post "evolution of the selfie" to show you how many times we take a picture to get it right!

That's the real shit.

I don't need to tell you how successful I am, because I don't consider myself to be successful yet. I'm making moves, but I'm just starting.

I've been through divorces, lost my kids, and got them back, I've gone through all kinds of dumb shit.

But I've remained positive throughout it.

Why?

Because I won't allow negativity to consume my life. I won't let it beat me. I find a way to see past it and find a positive look at a shit situation.

Trust me, there are days when I'm pissed off and I'm mad. But at the end of the day, that's life.

You only can control what you can control. That's something my baseball coach told me.

I can only control how I react to a situation. I can't control how you react, or how other people treat me.

For me, I just try and be a good dude.

That's not saying I do it every day. I fail. Often.

But I keep trying.

See, in life, you have to know WHY... You have to (at some point) truly know WHY you choose your daily path....

My WHY is easy.

I want to leave this world having had an impact, not on anyone in particular, more for my kids but I know residual effects can happen... others can be affected by this footprint of impression.

I want to be a positive influence for my kids, but would be blessed to help dads, veterans, anyone ... by showing my life. To show that I've had downfalls and I've picked myself back up. And I expect more downfalls and I'll pick myself back up again.

I'm raising my kids and I'm fucking it up; some days I feel like I am, at least, and other days I feel alright about it.

But I'm being open and honest with you. I'm showing you my heart. I'm giving you everything I possibly can.

Ultimately, life is a series of decisions. We make the best decisions we can based off the experiences we have gone through.

I share my story of failure and how I overcame sorrow to move on.

To give others an option they might not have seen.

In hopes that I can expose myself to the world so that the people in that world can live a braver existence.

So the Veteran can feel confident and face the world again...

So the mother can find the courage to attack life and provide for her child.

So that a father might find the strength to say "no" to work more and "YES" to family... to stand up and find happiness in himself and experience this beautiful thing we call life.

Because in 40 years whether anyone remembers me, I hope that I can be a casual effect that changes the course of history. If only for a single human.

There are a lot of famous people using their voice to push political agendas. They are influential and yet they don't know or understand the gravity of what they choose to say. I don't want to merely exist and provide no substance. If the world is going to follow me and for some reason give me a voice, I want to use it to empower more. I want to use it to help more.

I have two motives in life that really drive me. The first one should be pretty obvious because it is my family. I always imagine them watching me walk across some brightly-lit stage receiving an award, or recognition of some sort. In my mind I conjure the image of the proud looks on their faces.

I know the only way of making that thought a reality, is to work hard toward a goal. Which brings me to my second driving factor. I like to give myself small goals, or missions, if you will. Once I was out of the military, I felt there was no real direction. Of course there wasn't any direction, I no longer had superiors telling me what to do every minute of every day. Being on my own then, I wanted to do something with myself. Unlike some achievements in the military, there is no prebuilt path. There are no plans or directions that someone crafted before when they forged that same path. So, I created these small personal missions for myself and strive daily to achieve them. Something as simple as being a more affectionate dad, to something as difficult to getting back in shape have become my daily missions. I continue to hold myself accountable for my own self-improvement.

So, for my veterans reading this book of my mistakes and stories of overcoming them, I offer these pearls that I wish I had picked up before I separated. When you get out, you're in the best shape of your life, use that while you can. Live your life with purpose. Do real shit. Work. Work your ass off. Spend some money, save more of it. You need to realize as soon as possible that there is a whole world waiting for you back here in The States, and a life for you to make whatever you want out of it. Having a good, productive life is within reach if you just make the choices to go get it, and know yourself well enough to make those choices.

For all my other awesome friends that have given me the honor of reading this book, I have the following bits of advice to offer. Idle hands are the devil's playthings. That's no shit real talk. Stay busy. Maybe you are dealing with some tough things right now. That is an even bigger reason to stay busy. So do what it takes to not get into a position where you let self pity and doubt take over you. Everyday, look at yourself and do something that is taking you where you want to go, no matter how small it seems. But the more of these things you do, and the busier you are doing them, the faster you will get where you want to go.

The thing about hard work is, it pays off. No matter what you do, no matter who you work for, effort does not go unnoticed. It may not be by the right person, or get attention when you want it noticed, but someone sees it. If you think you're working hard and nobody is giving you a break, work harder. Keep going and let the end goal be your motivation.

What do I mean by that? Every human is a ship at sea. And every ship is sailing in one direction or another.

It's easy to stay on track when there's a guy screaming over your shoulder telling you how you are fucking things up. However you felt about being constantly evaluated in the military, at least some small part of you is going to miss that oversight in some way, at some point. There is something nice and comfortable about knowing exactly where you stand in terms of your work, all the time.

Back in The States you write your own ticket. There is no set purpose for how you are going to fit in to this great social machine. You have to carve that niche for yourself. I can't stress enough how important it is that you set goals for yourself and stay mission focused. The only difference now is that you pick the mission, and you are in charge of it being executed. So grab life by the balls and execute, execute, execute.

By the end of the year I should have hopefully become a better person, husband, and father by accomplishing these small missions. This has given me motivation to wake up the next day and keep grinding.

Setting these smaller step goals, and holding myself accountable to be the man I want to be for my family is my daily being now. And I will not deviate from my path of taking care of my family.

The fact of the matter is no person is going to give you motivation. You have to summon your own motivation and find out what is driving you to get to your next objective. So figure it out and take your steps every day to get to where you want to be. There is no magic formula to stay motivated or gathering any kind of motivation. It is an entirely self-induced and personal formula. Once you figure it out, don't let anything, or anyone, drag you off-course.

Remember that one day...

"Not sure why I thought of this today and you probably don't remember, but Cole Range was a Bitch! I remember it was especially hard on me mentally. I must have broke down like a dozen times over there. Anyways, we were all out in the road in the front leaning rest and the RI (Ranger Cadre) calls an amnesty period. Maybe 5 guys fell out. He said just one more drop and we'll end this smoke session. He promised us hot chow and a shower. Well I just about stood up. Seriously, I was over this shit at this moment. Right before I stood up, I kinda did a quick scan. I looked to my left and just a couple rows over, you had this insane fucking smile on your face. I know it was you because of that chin! You mumbled something under your breath. It was, "don't fucking quit" or maybe, "don't fucking do it!" I said to myself "this fucking guy does not give one single fuck!" You continued laughing under your breath. And I thought, well I don't give a fuck either. If this guy can SMILE while taking this punishment, how much of a pussy would I be if I threw it in here? Well turns out, I would go on to adopt this philosophy through every fucking school, every grueling march, every smoke session, basically every time it sucked. I know through your posts that you are battling some shit with your kids. It physically hurts to know a Ranger buddy is going through this. I sincerely hope it works out. Whether you meant it or not, that moment in Cole Range was responsible for a very big part of who I believe myself to be to this very day. I can't thank you enough. Just wanted to share that. Hope it was cheesy enough. Let me know if there is anything I can help with. Seriously, just let me know. Stay up brother."

Sent from my good friend-
Robbyjohn R. deGuzman

7 years service
UNCSB-JSA
Scout Sniper PLT
Ranger Battalion 04-06
Recce/Sniper PLT
1/294 GUARNG Scout Sniper PLT

Let me start with this and I will explain as best I can… You never really know, at least I never really know, the power and energy you possess for others around you. I never realized my silly mindset I carried with me throughout hard training could have a positive impact on my peers. My thought was, you can always look around and see someone feeling sorry for themselves. And if you can't find someone? Then it's you feeling sorry for yourself… The idea made me smile... the idea gave my energy…I would recite in my head… YOU CAN'T BREAK ME… over, and over, and over, with a smile on my face and doing everything within my power to believe those words…

This message was emailed to me by a Ranger buddy, early in the morning on the day I lost my kids in a painful custody battle. I made a vague post on social media about the pain I was feeling that day. Not knowing if I would be able to afford hiring a lawyer and fighting to get them back was truly killing me inside. This gentleman sent that story in his message to me. He didn't realize at that time, or ever since, how much of an impact it had. And how it also motivated me to keep moving. I had somehow, through the agonizing court process, forgotten the very characteristic that got me to that critical point in my life. I'm so grateful to this day, that he took the time on THAT day, to remind me of who I was, and that I gave him some of my motivation. I'm very proud to share it with you all now, in my latest show of motivation. Stay positive, smile in the face of adversity, and keep moving forward.

I dusted myself off and appealed the court's decision. Two months later, I won back full custodial rights of my four children.

Chapter Six

Balance

"My body-type is the kind where you can tell I work out here and there, but I also never said no to a taco."
#Balance

I look at him and wish my life was that simple...

He looks at me and wishes his life was this exciting...

I talked to a guy today that felt he never lived an exciting life. Never felt he had really done anything.

But I envied him. He still had his wife, his kids, and gets to enjoy them everyday after he leaves his ordinary job...

I, on the other hand, I have a crazy exciting job and I go home alone and don't get to see my kids everyday.

At the end of this life when I am on my death bed, I hope someone will be there to hold my hand as I go...

He will have a room full of that...

This was one of my journal entries from 2016. On one of my many flights, I sat next to a man who started some small talk. Based on his general appearance, I could tell he wasn't a physical man, he was working on his computer and asked me what I did for a living. I told him I worked for the Border Patrol. He became more intrigued and kept digging with more questions. We talked about my deployments and what it's like to hunt another human being. This gentleman couldn't get enough of hearing me tell him about my life. He seemed to be in awe of what I have experienced, and it made me feel good, for the moment. Then I asked about his life. He worked in IT and was married with two kids. He worked a typical nine-to-five job and was home every night with his family. He envied me for my life. I envied him for his. One life, gives you the opportunity to be involved in your family's life. The other, albeit exciting, can be hard on a family. I was newly single, and was flying back to Texas from a short trip to visit my kids. I questioned if my life choices have been wrong all these years, and wondered if I will die alone for having made these choices.

Life is about balance. As the driver in your life, you must identify your own brand of balance. What are the aspects in your life that make you happy? What things make you happy when you go and do them? Obviously not everyone will have the same happy things as me. Maybe you have pets, like dogs that you totally love and adore. Perhaps you are single, and enjoy traveling because you're free of attachments.

It doesn't matter who we are or what kind of success we seek. Each of us has that thing (or things) that drives us and makes us happy. Whatever it is you derive your happiness from, there is a balance that needs to be maintained. It is only when that balance is on point that your life will tend to run a lot more smoothly. I think people misconstrue 'balance' for inclusion. I've found balance to be achieved by the choices you make. And like any adult choices, that often means some sacrifices must be made. Choosing what NOT TO DO, or what areas of your life to place fewer resources, is just as important as choosing TO DO certain things.

To maintain my personal mental balance and health, I do a lot of self-evaluation and reflection. My own form of meditation, I guess. I look at my life and its current state, and see if I am still living a life that I can be proud of. Have I kept my integrity and dignity? Have I made choices that were for the better of my family? Am I being fulfilled in this path I am on? Am I inspired daily to wake up and keep moving forward? If for any reason I am in a position where I feel like I am not happy mentally I must break down the reasons why, and how can I fix it.

"Say YES to family daily, and NO to work more often."

While I was serving in the Border Patrol I found myself in a position where I was about to miss my daughter's birthday because I was called into work to be on a task force that was going chase down two recently escaped convicts. This was national news, and I was going to be a part of it. Every three-letter agency in the United States was looking for these two escaped criminals.

Afterward, I made the tough choice to leave the Border Patrol after seven years to spend more time with my family. Leaving that environment was an agonizing decision for me, but I was ready to be more involved in my kids' lives. I longed to be more involved in my kids' lives. I needed to be there for more of everything I was missing.

Mentally, I needed to make that choice. It takes me back to my second oldest child's birthday. This beautiful baby girl was born to me in 2005. I was fortunate to have witnessed her birth, but have not been as lucky with many other events in her life. Work has always had other plans for me. The Idea of missing another one of my daughters' birthdays terrified me. She was growing accustomed to her dad being gone. That was a shame. Of course in some cases it was out of my control based on my career choices. This job paid the bills, it provided a comfortable lifestyle for my family. That was all I felt I needed to do to justify my lack of existence and presence in their daily lives. I knew this was wrong. In the core of my being I knew I was wrong. I knew they deserved more, but for some reason I couldn't come to terms with what I would have to do to be home more for them. I believed that I couldn't afford to find a new job, and the debt was stacking up because I was living well outside my means.

So, I was stuck. I didn't have be in Special Operations. I could easily have moved to a line officer position, but I was still addicted to the lifestyle. I was seven days into the search with my team and decided to ask my supervisor if I could head home early for my daughter's birthday.

The manhunt we were for the escaped prison inmates of New York, plagued the Northeast in the summer of 2015. I was a part of the unit that tracked down those fugitives. My team leader there, took the fatal shot that killed Richard Sweat.

That night, after we completed our mission, the team did some Karaoke. We had a good time fucking up a bunch of random songs and having some drinks to debrief those past two days. They didn't know it but that was my last hoorah with the boys. I finally made the choice to leave my team in the fight, while I tended to my family. I was tired of being the kids' paycheck. I needed to be more relevant in their daily lives. I spent almost fifteen years training other people's kids, and it was now time to train and mentor my own.

My family matters. Not just having a family, but actually watching these kids grow and having someone to share those memories with, matters. As I venture into the acting world now, I definitely face the chance of being totally consumed by it. I tend to go all-in with everything I do. And that means I must make a conscious decision to say NO to some very interesting opportunities. We talk as a family about each project and determine if it is worth it for the family. And no matter the opportunity, if we both don't totally agree, then I say no. This is my own version of checks and balances.

I think most people have a spiritual outlet of some sort. And like most human details, that spiritual outlet or connection is as individual as it is personal. That deeply personal spiritual relationship and experience is important for life balance. Your 'because' may not be the same as mine. But what I live for, is my children. Spiritually, I lead by example and I want to mentor my children as best as I can. In my case, I have my relationship with my God, and that's all I really need to say about that.

There was a time in my life when I would laugh at other people's fears of physical activity. The idea of total exhaustion was a myth to me, as a younger man. I was in amazing shape once upon a time; I guess that applies to most of us. I didn't have to count calories or worry about how a shirt looked on me, and whether it covered my gut or not. I see pictures of myself that people post on social media, where I didn't have the presence of mind to suck it in before they said cheese. That moment is then frozen for the rest of time, and put on display for public consumption just puts salt in the wound. It's embarrassing, humiliating, and worst of all, depressing. It then piles on to the pressure to just give up, try to get accustomed to being a fat guy, and get used to seeing that image of myself.

More and more these days, it's like I woke up in someone else's body. What happened? Where did I go wrong? I find myself out of breath when I play with my kids. But fast food is convenient, easy, and slides into my busy life like a puzzle piece. So, I buy bigger clothes. But still a tick develops where I find myself constantly pulling at my shirt, so it doesn't hug my belly, giving temporary camouflage to the monument of my shame. Out in the world, one might see me as a confident man walking tall and smiling at everyone. While inside, a war wages. A battle where I am too embarrassed to go swimming with my kids because people might see me with my shirt off and laugh.

My family, they never find anything wrong with me. They continue to think Big Papi is a badass. Little do they know I fear I might not have the stamina in the event they truly need me. I tell myself, it's harder on me because I was in such great shape, and it wasn't so long ago. I tell myself it's because I went through a bad divorce, and a long custody battle. It's harder because I had a major move, a new job, and a new life challenge. It's been an emotional rollercoaster. A rollercoaster that I boarded wearing size large, and exited busting the seams of a double-extra-large. I tell myself this isn't my problem, that it's just life. But these are all just excuses.

I wrote this about a year after leaving the Border Patrol. Still struggling with fitness, still wishing I could get back to the good old days of being muscled and lean. But this current Big Papi body, as much as I dislike it, is part of my balance. I know if I dedicate my life to my fitness it will lose time somewhere else. By no means am I saying other things are more important than my health but what I am saying is, it's okay not to be ripped. In my WORK/ LIFE balance system, I find time to go to the gym, but I'm also ok with missing a few days, or weeks. I have so many other endeavors which I feel fit better now for the comfort of family and career balance. I am still building my empire, and once that's done I will focus on my abs.

As a little boy, one of the first things you learn about life is that you will always be stronger when you are part of a team. After all, we are pack animals; it is how we have survived for this long. People are hard-wired with this sense of community not because we enjoy it, but because it is necessary. Popular sports mimic the hunt, the battle, or the war, in one way or another. Execution of strategy; working together to outsmart, outplay, and out-hustle the other guys in the different color uniforms, is how the games are played. Finding the best use of your power and focusing it collectively where it can do the most damage to your opponent is the heart of team sports and it is the soul of war.

Years ago as I sat in that big house all alone, the house that was filled with the memories of a life long gone, I concluded I didn't need to turn the lights on anymore. The pitch-black room was fitting for my state of mind. This was my reward for setting big goals and accomplishing them; it was my prize for being good at a job many couldn't do, or didn't even want. You find out after a while that filling every breath you have with this sexy high-speed lifestyle isn't as cool as it seems. And giving all of yourself to it will draw the ironic cruelty of life leaving you with seemingly nothing.

I had friends who tried to warn me, who had seen this coming, as I put this job above everything else. But it was much simpler for me, I was the right size peg for this hole. Why else would God put this in my heart? He must have a plan for me. Whatever that plan may have been, I wasn't willing to change myself. I had tried so many times. They say the path of the warrior is a solitary one. You work so hard to climb the ladder and accomplish impossible achievements. But in the end, there is nobody to share it with. Having nobody to share your successes with you ultimately takes all those awesome feelings of victory, out of them.

When I returned home to the real world, I found myself standing on level ground with people who had taken a completely different path with their time on this earth. Back at home, I wondered about the future; in fifty years on my death bed, I hoped someone would be there to hold my hand when I passed. My neighbor didn't worry about things like that. He would always have a room full of people around to grieve and celebrate life with, and those who could comfort him at the end.

Who would be there to hold my hand? I had made choices my whole life thinking that they were good for the team, but the aftermath had proven quite different. Somehow the more I focused I was on the team, the more selfish I became from the perspective of my family. The guy next door went to college, got married, and raised a family. He had seen his children being born, he had seen their first steps, and he had heard their first words. What had I heard from my dark, empty house? I was missing the fact that I was completely focused on the well-being of the wrong team.

Balance is never spoken of in our community because it isn't relevant, not to the mission. The mission is about today. Feelings and other bullshit are for later. The key is to focus on our training and live through today. Everything else is secondary. This is a necessary evil for Special Operations units. Not only SOF in the military, but Law Enforcement Officers as well. Wives don't normally understand why it is so hard for us to say 'no' to our units. They aren't haunted with the mission they missed because of an injury. They are not stuck living with the idea that if they were on that mission, things could have gone differently.

As I stand over him, I no longer look at him with hate or fear

For he is no longer my enemy but my brother

As we are all brothers in the eyes of the Lord,

But today,

I was the instrument of his death.

By Ricardo Barraza

I struggled hard with coming home. I had spent every waking moment with these men. During that time you push away any emotional ties with your wife and kids and rebuild that safety net of emotion with the soldiers you are surrounded by. To return home and have to revert back just seemed impossible. My mind was still wired for the mission. Do whatever you're ordered; kill, capture, life and death, and dumping huge doses of pure adrenaline. Where was that excitement at home; where was the adventure? You're left with a wife who doesn't know you and kids who knew just enough to forget. It's hard to admit but it's the truth.

When you look back, the love you have for your team seems almost greater than that which you have for your own family. Guilt permeates your being, even though you know in your bones, it was the only way.

When you are great at something, everything else seems to get the leftovers.

Coming to terms with that as a fact of life instead of carrying it as baggage can be the most important phase of turning that switch to the off position. For me, everything seemed to happen in phases. There was a warming up period and reconnection before I found my way back to the action.

Now I am on my third marriage and I'm happy, and it's not by mistake. My happiness is the result of finally committing to making the changes I needed to make. I have turned down some jobs. And I have made a conscious decision to be home more. And I'm not just physically home, but I'm also fully mentally present at home. I force myself to be in uncomfortable situations like working behind a desk and not always being a grunt. I'm determined to succeed at changing the ratio from brawn to brains.

I make the effort for romance and have discovered the little things that build the connection with my wife that will last forever. I screw that up all the time, but she knows I'm trying. And that is what matters, that she sees I am working at it. Sometimes I miss sleep altogether, just so I can have a few moments alone. A little bit of time to myself without sacrificing anybody else's time. That sacrifice is the difference between my other marriages, and why this one works.

I haven't always had a sense of balance. I realized how badly I needed it after losing my ex-wife and my kids several years ago. There were a few reasons for the divorce, but I know my being gone did not help. You see, before, when I was gone it wasn't an issue to me because I was doing what a father does for his family. I was the breadwinner and the sole provider. In typical man-of-the-house fashion I missed births and birthdays, ballet recitals, sports games, and talent shows. I missed practically everything that is cherished by the average civilian parent. Yet I was completely numb to it. That's not to say I didn't care. But because I felt such a profound purpose with my objective, whatever it was at the time, I didn't connect it with those lost moments. Most wives won't ever really understand it. And if they do understand, they only have so much tolerance for it before they break.

Everyone has a breaking point, no matter how sweet and gentle they might be. She has a point where being alone isn't worth the person that comes home to her. I have seen great relationships fall apart, mainly because the wife felt her husband didn't care. It is an empty and lonely way to live. The men in these relationships never feel fully engaged. Family is important but the mission always comes first. Without the mission the family would not exist. Now, I finally see that to accomplish a successful family, the focus isn't on completing any particular objective. The victory happens the second you show up at home and give your family your full heart.

Things had normalized for me. I was a federal agent. It gave me the rush I needed to feel fulfilled, and still got me home most nights for dinner. I saw my kids every day and I was able to spend the time with them that I missed while they were babies. I got to see them struggle with the lessons of life the same way I did. I could see them developing into the men and women they would eventually become; their personalities and talents ever-evolving. I was able to watch my sons playing baseball. They practiced and worked with their team as they refined the skill-set required to run with the pack. I wonder still if they will follow in my footsteps. Reflecting back to a time when my dad watched me learning the same skills, I also wonder if he thought about his time in the Marine Corps and envisioned my future when he was watching me.

It is my wish for every person that reads this book to take away this lesson, find you balance. The path of least resistance is always the most tempting. Unfortunately, it isn't always the best or most productive path. Finding balance while important, is not going to be easy for every person. Of course it will be easier for some, but for others there may be some struggle, and some difficult decisions to make. Figuring out what your priorities are and reorganizing your life around them in order to be happy will never be a decision you regret. No man lays on his deathbed and says, 'if only I had spent more time at work.' Time is the one thing we can't buy, and we can never get back once it has passed. So don't waste any more time, find your balance and live life with happiness at the top of the list. If you're lucky, and you do things right, there will be plenty of loved ones around to hold your hand at the end of this life.

Chapter Seven

Fear

Become the Lighthouse... - By Vincent Vargas

You want to know the answers and why it's so hard, why these waves keep knocking you down and why you keep falling apart...

You need to rise above the waves... or hold your breath until it has passed... you can't quit this life and drown in the aftermath...

Stand tall and let the waves hit hard... it's inevitable, your small cuts will become scarred

There's no stopping the pain and cold it leaves behind, take in that deep breath knowing that what is coming, is by design

With little success and ease of breath come bitterness and

pain from failures in vain...

As the waves crash again and again

You will lose more than you win... keep standing don't fall and don't give in...

Hold! Hold! Hold without fear, you can see the waves coming now... while relationships disappear

People grow older and bodies get tired... keep standing proud... while the world around you expires.

For you were just a pebble in the sand, you managed to stack yourself higher and higher with your own hand...

Stone after stone your walls grow tall, it's going to take one hell of a hit to make you fall

As the waves crash now... they seem to hit with less power... for you have now become the beacon of light....

Way up high in the tower

People will come to you and ask, how... How can I become this strong... and not crumble to powder

Endure the waves as they crash down and you become doused

Build from your pain.. become the lighthouse...

Note: I wrote this poem for those who seem to always have the hardest of lives. Sometimes life is unfair, and the only thing you can do is learn from the mistakes. Find a way to heal. Eventually you will be the one people turn to for help and how to handle hard life situations. You become the lighthouse the guide others to safety.

Fear:(as defined by Merriam-Webster) a distressing emotion aroused by impending danger, evil, pain, etc., whether the threat is real or imagined; the feeling or condition of being afraid.

The most intimate moment in my life wasn't in a bedroom or even during sex. It was in a ten-by-six cement block.

I was working at a prison in September of 2007. I was two months out of the Army and I was younger than most of my colleagues. My body was in top shape compared to my coworkers, and I was still full of fire from the uncomfortable transition out of the military. I had just about one month's worth of night shifts on the floor as a corrections officer.

I was always willing to get into a scrap, fighting never bothered me. On that day around one o'clock in the morning, I was called on the intercom.

"Vargas please report to the Response team room."

I knew it was going to be a cell extraction. I was nervous and excited all at the same time. When I got to the room there were already seven guys there getting suited up. The Captain on duty pulled me to the side and asked if I was ok with being the team leader.

I too-readily said, "Fuck yeah!"

I looked around at my team of misfits and started breaking them down, asking, "Who is prior service? Who has done this before? Who wants to be the shield man?"

By the count of guys getting dressed out, I could already tell this was a two-man job, maybe more. Since I was the team leader I decided I should try to subdue the big guy. I would learn soon enough he was doing time for murder.

I asked the Captain about the inmates. They were in permanent segregation. One was in for murder, and it was one of the ugliest murders I have ever read about. The other was in for attempted murder. Both were locals from a nearby reservation. I was told they had both changed their diets to Kosher diets a month before, so they could collect the oranges.

With the peels of all their Kosher oranges they were able to make prison hooch. Evidently they were able to make a lot of it, because they were pretty drunk. Once the corrections officer noticed it during an inspection, he ordered them to cuff up so he could collect and confiscate the contraband. The inmate refused his order. After a few more failed attempts, the CO called the Captain to control the situation. Once this happened the inmate started destroying his cell. He was breaking everything that could be broken.

For some reason they had porcelain toilets and sinks in the cells at this time. It didn't take long before all that was broken and the small window in the back of the cell was also busted out. That was what spun up the midnight shift response team.

On my team I had a few guys that were as young as I was, but a few really big guys as well. Overall though, everyone was pretty new. We lined up and filmed our portion of the extraction for legal reasons. Once we lined up, I started going up and down the line giving them the details of what I can see in the room through the toilet paper the inmates had pasted to the window.

No shit, it was like we had fucking teenage mutant ninja inmates. When you see this for the first time it is no joke and really scary. They wore knee and elbow pads fashioned from cut up sandals. They had body protection with layers of wrapped sheets, and socks filled with broken pieces of porcelain. I couldn't see the floor from my vantage point. I know now if I could have seen the floor it might have made a difference in the method I used to approach the whole situation. This was because the prisoners had buttered the floor with a healthy coating of soap to make us slip and fall upon entry.

First, the captain introduced chemical munitions into the room through the food trap. At the same time, they threw out what was left of the sink, hitting me, and then the captain, in the legs. We closed the trap and I heard the sound of a can being pushed between something. I would later realize that they shoved the can of OC CS(professional pepper spray) mix outside the back window they had earlier broken.

The captain heard exactly what I heard and decided it was good to go in since they threw the one thing they had as a weapon at us. I didn't help because at this point I was reminded of the anticipation of getting ready to breach a door and start fucking dudes up. So, I gave the old thumbs up. Mind you I had only been working here for a month, so who was I to say when to enter a fucking cell. I guess the joke was on me.

As we approach a cell with two guys, the first two men on the team are shield guys. Their job is to pin and control the inmate, so the others can get control of the inmate's extremities. When the two big boys made the initial entry, they both hit the deck. The soap proved to be effective. So there I was, the third man to enter the room. I knew I was going to have to subdue the big guy who was the murderer, so I kept pushing forward. I took the most direct route to him. As I got closer everything became a haze of slow motion. I could actually see the asshole swing that sock at me and me not feeling anything, but thinking, 'what the fuck is he doing?' It took me a second to realize I was getting beaten with a sock that had some kind of hard object inside it. The sonofabitch was trying to kill me with a sock full of broken toilet bowl. At that moment I realized I was about to scrap with a drunk murderer who was in for life. He had absolutely nothing to lose and I was just entertainment to him.

I decided right then, fuck the rules- it's survival time. I grabbed his shit and started to strike this fucker with everything I could. After about four solid blows to his face we both slipped on the floor and I landed on top of him. I "continued to strike pressure point locations until the inmate was following my orders." This is something that is drilled into you during the training class. You are never allowed to strike an inmate in the face. It is only acceptable to strike pressure point locations. I obviously decided to throw all that out the window once I felt I was in serious mortal danger. As I wrote my memo explaining the event, you bet your ass I said "continued to strike pressure point locations until the inmate was following my orders." And "I assisted the inmate to the floor gently until the rest of the team was in the room and able to control both individuals." The way he ended up on the floor and the speed it took to get there, is clearly a matter of which of us you ask.

I was completely okay with getting fired for my actions. I made that decision when I closed-fist punched him in his face. I used the quote as I did because while writing the report, these are the terms you have to use to sound more professional. This was also the voice going through my head as I continued to punch this guy with no regrets. By then, the rest of the team was in the room and able to control both individuals. The inmate ended up with a dislocated shoulder when we both hit the floor.

After the incident he went to the prison medical department and from there he was taken to the hospital. I was evaluated and had some bruising starting to show from the sock beating.

Why do I say this was the most intimate moment of my life? I say it because in those moments, I was at my most vulnerable. My life was exposed and in mortal danger, and those things made it intimate.

Experiencing true, deep vulnerability is an emotional experience. I had spent that last four years of my life kicking-in doors with the comfort of a rifle in my hands to protect my team and myself. That in itself is form of life insurance. It is effectively a security blanket and the comfort needed in combat. But if the war were hypothetical hand-to-hand combat-only war, I don't believe we would have had as many people volunteer to serve. It's like any Special Operations unit now. You have guys who love to train and fight. And then you have the guys whom, if given a choice, would never train.

I enjoy training in the gym. I have always loved sparring and competing, yet I was completely overwhelmed at the reality of that moment. Fighting is fun until you realize it may actually be a life and death situation. There is no sentiment that can compare to the intimacy of those moments when life is given, or nearly taken away.

Fear is a funny beast. A simple thing as an emotion built into us as human beings to protect us from the danger stimulus, has the ability to absolutely cripple us in so many facets of our lives. Fear can be extremely beneficial, if you learn how to listen to it and how to respond properly when it is triggered.

Some would call fear a liar, since it often leads to exaggerated or unnecessary emotional and physical responses. The move is knowing when to listen to the warnings and take appropriate action, or realizing that your fear is effectively making a mountain out of a mole hill. Thousands of books have been written about this subject. And one of the most prominent among those authors is Gavin de Becker. He actually considers fear a gift because it is the one emotion that will help us preserve our life and protect those around us. I tend to agree with him.

Learn how to mitigate your fear. Figure out the times when you need to stare it down and call it a liar as you walk toward the chaos. And separate the times when you need to listen closely to fear and decide if it is time for fight or flight. Most situations you will be facing will involve the former, because fear can be a liar. And facing it will make you grow in ways you have never imagined.

Ralph Waldo Emerson said, "God will not have His work made manifest by cowards." That doesn't mean that only the fearless or apathetic will be charged with doing important things, not even close. It means that the greatest things will be done by ordinary men who when faced with great fear, will go forward in spite of it. Courage is not the embodiment of the brave who are never afraid. Courage is being afraid, but summoning the intestinal fortitude to face the obstacle anyway in order to conquer our objectives. Fear itself is a good thing. Do not underestimate its value in your life or spectrum of emotions. It's there for a reason, learn to harness it and use it to your advantage.

Intimate: (as defined by Merriam-Webster) adjective - very private; closely personal

Chapter Eight

Acceptance

"Because for someone to say you have potential is an insult. Potential is just the procrastination of greatness."

All I can be is me...

I don't have to show a face

I can be a failure in this empty place

As long as I don't stray I am proud to show you my way...

This is me, this is who I am

Someone who fails time and time again

I get up and I know this life won't just flow

I get up, and keep on going toward my goal...

Because I am only one thing that's all I can be, I am just me

Honest, real and full of insecurities...

This poem is a self-reflection of checks and balances. I sometimes have to remind myself I don't have to be anything other than myself. It's easy to be influenced by others. It's easy to be something other people want you to be and stray from the honest truth to be what we are.

L ife can sneak up and kick you right in the nuts. Your wife left you for another man, your parent passed away, your friend took his or her own life...

Sometimes life just deals out a shit stack of cards.

Devin K. Peguero was killed in training on December 16th, 2004. We went to Basic training in October 2003. We became friends early on during in-processing. He was another big Mexican kid from LA and we just hit it off. While in basic we were in different platoons, but we always tried to check in on each other from time to time. We went to Airborne School together and stood right next to each other during formation.

This is really when our friendship grew stronger. We knew Ranger Indoctrination Program wasn't going to be easy and the last thing we wanted was to let ourselves get out of shape while in Airborne School. We made a pact to get smoked all day and we would do it together.

One of us would always repeat the phrase, "I got you Ranger buddy" while we smiled because our plans were working.

Being "smoked" is a term used in the military to refer physical fitness punishment because of a disciplinary action. The more we behaved like smartasses to the NCOs in our platoon, the more they smoked us. I remember the NCOs telling us we weren't ready for RIP and we would never make it as Rangers because we weren't disciplined enough. We had a plan and it was working.

Once we in-processed into RIP, the cadre gave us the weekend off and warned us of a PT Test on Monday morning. Like any respectable youngsters with a few dollars in their accounts, we went to have a few beers. We ended up getting into a fight with some actual Army Rangers. Not the smartest move we have ever made, but youth and testosterone can cloud the thinking. In the best interest of our careers we practiced our evade and escape tactics, and hid in the bed of a random pickup truck.

Monday morning at formation Devin was called up to the front. We all knew we were fucked. Somehow, they knew it was us. By the grace of God, they were only calling him up because he was missing his ID card. They recycled Devin to the next class. Before leaving to Washington, I told him to get through it and I will see him at 2nd Battalion.

When I came back from my first deployment, one of the first people I saw at the chow hall was Devin. I was so damn excited to see he had made it. We talked about life and caught each other up on things that were happening in our lives. I invited him to my house a few weeks later for a home cooked meal and some beers.

The day before he was supposed to come over I received a call saying Devin was killed in training. It's not something that happens often but it is the sad reality of training with live rounds. There were a lot of things that went wrong and a lot of people have paid the price for this tragic event, so I don't want this to be about that.

Devin wanted to be an Army Ranger. He believed in this dream and he achieved it. For reasons I will never understand, he was taken from us too soon. He did everything right. He never quit, and he lived the Ranger Creed. In this case, life was not fair for him and for his family. For me, I lost a great friend whose incredible smile, even today I can still see when I close my eyes and wander back to those days.

It's crazy how the world is sometimes. I was sent to Ranger School sometime near September, and all I remember was, if I could graduate without being recycled, I would graduate December 16th, 2005. If that wasn't motivation for me to kick ass and finish on-time, I don't know what would be. I was able to earn my Ranger tab as scheduled, and in my heart I earned one for Devin that day, as well. Love you, brother.

Are any of those things mentioned above a reason to fail? Will you just allow some random thing to force you to give in to a victim mindset, or can you rise above the flame? All these examples are fucking terrible. Some of the worst shit you would never want to experience in a lifetime. I've been there, done that and I didn't even get a shirt for it! I have personally dealt with my share of surprises and life changing mishaps. In all situations listed above, one can't get past the reality of the situation until they have accepted it has happened, and it's one-hundred percent out of their control. Once you can tell yourself to accept that a situation is real and there is no changing the current outcome, then you can begin to heal from the hurt and pain you are left with. Only then will you be able to grow past it.

When I first got to my unit in the Army there was a high energy NCO (Non- commissioned officer) who was in charge of Alpha company while the boys were deployed to Afghanistan. We stayed in the common area until the platoons came back to pick and choose which soldiers they wanted. It's the Ranger version of an NFL draft. Or an Army Ranger iteration of school-yard pick-em, take your pick.

The platoon knew where they were missing power and needed to fortify their unit. Most of the big guys like me were almost immediately jammed into a weapons team where they would have to manage a crew served weapon called a 240 Bravo. Or you might be sent to Anti-Tank where you trained to carry, fire, and jump out of planes with a beast of a rocket launcher. I was one of those unfortunate souls who was picked to carry the weight. Others were fortunate to go directly to a line team and kick-in doors. That was every Infantryman's dream.

This high energy NCO, or Blue as we came to call him, would wake us up randomly in the middle of the night, quiz us with some crazy weird trivia and leave. Growing up, my father would come into my room to wake me up early in the morning for yard duties, so it was a familiar sound when he came charging into the room. Even though my father was trying to teach me about responsibilities, and this guy had other motives, it still seemed somewhat familiar. I would jump out of my cot as fast as I could because the repercussions for being the last one out of bed could be painful.

Every time I would jump out of bed he would say "damnit I knew I liked you, you are going to go far" and then he would spout off a random quote. "Did you know Ty Cobb was the best baseball player that has ever lived?"

Baseball was another thing we had in common. After my first deployment Blue and I became closer. He would check on me from time to time and see how I was advancing in my military career.

In 2006, one of our friends was killed in Iraq. By this time, I knew SGT Blue was struggling with an addiction to painkillers. Being that I was of lesser rank, I honestly wasn't sure how to approach this. I was a twenty-five year old SPC (E-4) wanting to help a twenty-six year old SGT

(E-5). I didn't want to offend him, and maybe I was over reacting. Or maybe it was none of my god-damn business.

We were assigned to the funeral detail. I knew how hard this was for me and I could only imagine how hard this was to be for him. I found myself in his hotel room helping him get dressed, and helping him organize his meds for the day. I remember asking him if he had it under control. I knew at the time he was hung up on a few things that happened during his time as a Ranger. Missions he missed that lead to some serious casualties, and now this, all haunted his daily existence. He blamed himself for not being healthy enough to deploy when he lost a close friend. You hear that time heals all wounds, but I now know this isn't the truth. Time only heals those who can accept life's plan. It is a brutal reality that we cannot control.

SGT Blue called me years later while I was in the Border Patrol, asking me to quit so I could join him on a contract overseas. I was tempted, but the voice coming across the phone had a familiar slur. I was contacted by his family a few days later that SGT Blue had overdosed on painkillers.

It is in a moment like this when you must make a conscious decision to grow.

Far too many times people are held up on the idea of disbelief, sucked under by feelings of guilt and depression.

You can get so buried by these intangible burdens, that you don't see a way to get relief from the pain. In these moments we all feel broken beyond repair. I can assure you that your life will get better. You will heal, and you will find happiness again. You have to decide to become better, learn from this experience and move past it.

From the deaths of my friends from the military, I have been given motivation to live my best life. I am not as likely to drink on the anniversary date to the point where I get so trashed I punch a wall. We have all done this in some form. We have all seen the occasions when we hurt ourselves or have taken a crazy risk because we felt loss or hurt, or we were just overwhelmed. In a way it seems we are trying to put the pain on our ourselves because of how much we still hurt. It is as if we can take the pain from our insides and bring it to the outside where it will hurt less. We have this weird mindset for our self-destructive actions.

Maybe we provoke these feelings so that we can feel justified that we still have a life. It is hard to explain and break down, and definitely not the medical answer. But this is the only explanation I can come up with as to why I would try to drink myself into a sobbing baby. I just wanted to show my brothers how much they meant to me. I wanted them to see my pain in some way. I wanted to world to know I was still broken from my past experiences. I wouldn't let go of any of it... because if I did, how was that showing how much these brilliant men meant to me?

I was wrong. If there is a heaven, they definitely aren't looking down excited about how many bottles I am putting down in a night. They wouldn't be smiling saying, "Fuck yes, he is living his best life!" I imagine the opposite is actually true. Now I believe they would be gravely disappointed. And that disappointment is not something I can live with while I'm still here. There is power in saying it and changing it. I was wrong.

Here is the truth. I am happier now. I have accepted their deaths. I have accepted my divorce. I have accepted those who have taken their own lives due to unforeseen events. I can only LIVE... I can only move forward from here and find a way to be better. I can love better. I can work harder. I can do more. I can completely become a new person once I have accepted those losses.

Until you can accept where you are and where you've failed, there will always be excuses. Acceptance allows people to make changes. It's the conduit that pushes you forward.

Control what you can control and let go of what you can't. You have to make peace with life. There is no point in arguing with reality, because what is, just is.

I am told all the time how great of a father I am. That statement is always hard to swallow. I know the people saying these words are only seeing recent years. And seeing it all through the colored glass of social media, at that. But no one has seen the years I missed, the years when I didn't really matter. The times when I was proud to call myself a father but was missing almost everything of importance in my precious children's lives. Now people see something completely different on the other side. I try not to miss anything. I take them to school and pick them up most of the year. I am home for the wrestling tournaments and the baseball games. I am sitting at the kitchen table helping the kids with homework I can barely figure out myself. This whole change of perspective came from accepting my wrongs and actively choosing to right them. I was making every excuse to not be home because work was always less work than being a dad. The fact of the matter is, it's exhausting. It's emotional, it's hard, and it's a different struggle for every child. It was just easier for me back then to justify work over family. My silent vow to them to be a more present father won't be broken, no matter where my career now takes me.

You can only change once you acknowledge there is reason for change. Something profound and unfortunate can happen for you to see the need for change, or you can evaluate your life and accept you are currently in the wrong.

Accept that you are not perfect. Be okay with your

imperfections and work toward being as close to perfect as you can get. "Aim small miss small" was what we said in the Army. So work toward being as perfect as you can manage. Falling short of that is at least near perfect.

"Every action has an equal and opposite reaction."

Once you have accepted change is necessary you will inevitably have to accept the sacrifices that are needed to make that change. What's that change really worth to you? What about the end result? Are you willing to lose your family if you don't change? Are you willing to start all over? Are you willing to eat ramen noodles for months until you can get back on your feet in the direction you want your life to go?

I walked away from the Border Patrol hoping the pay from one of my companies would keep me afloat until I got going with my next venture. I came to realize that isn't how the business world works. I was drowning in debt and I had to accept that I would lose my house if I didn't do something, fast. I was lucky enough to find a job selling cars in El Paso, Texas, and late at night I was an Uber driver. I knew what I was sacrificing. I was choosing work over the kids for the time being, because I didn't want to lose my house. At that point, shelter was the priority. I evaluated my life and decided I could still recover from these circumstances, and I made a choice. This would take time away from the family, but it was the necessary decision to keep moving forward. So there I was, selling fucking cars and giving late-night Uber rides to complete strangers with some incredible conversations.

After about six months I was able to stop driving Uber. Eventually I also walked away from being a car salesman. I was able to find other avenues of making money, so I could be home more.

Now I prepare for those hard times that are coming.

It's a fact of life that you will face hardships. Are you ready? Have you war-gamed those days? Have you visualized them? Have you spent time emotionally preparing, physically readying, and financially securing?

I have been doing this for years, it is something I learned while I was growing up. Fighting was common growing up with a twin sister and a father whose life revolved around boxing. A big part of being ready for a fight is knowing every possible outcome. Visually seeing every single potential possibility. If my opponent moves left, I move right. If I am hurt I need to hold on or take a knee for the eight-count.

I took this same idea and have made it my life's plan to be prepared for everything. If you want to know how thorough I am with my contingency planning, I have planned for almost any situation that life can bring at me, from an alien invasion to having a new baby.

On every road I drive to every door I enter, I make it a point to have a plan of action for the worst-case scenario.

This keeps me mentally ready for anything. Yes, I think of some of the worst shit to help me emotionally and mentally be ready for it. I don't want to get caught off-guard. I believe that some of the hardest things to handle are the things you would have never expected.

So think of every outcome and possibility. Get your answers there. Figure out a plan so that in the event shit happens you are somewhat prepared for it.

Accept that while you can't control every outcome, you can prepare for many of the circumstances. Accept your limitations, be they financial or physical. Take the time and effort to work around them or just figure out solutions to overcome some of them to the best of your ability. Buddhists believe that acceptance is the path to enlightenment. I have learned over all these years that they are onto something. Accepting all the things that you can't change forces you to grow in ways that you didn't before imagine. And once you force your mind to accept those things, you will be able to rise to a new level in your thinking and your being. And eventually, that enlightenment will lead you to happiness. The ultimate destination is always happiness. So do some real introspection and scrutinize what in your life you are fighting and not accepting. That will help you see what is keeping you from growing.

Preparation: (as defined by Merriam-Webster) noun- any proceeding, experience, or the like considered as a mode of preparing for the future.

Acceptance: (as defined by Merriam-Webster) the act of taking or receiving something offered.

Enlightenment: (as defined by Merriam-Webster) the act of intellectual or spiritual light to; instruct; impart knowledge to another.

Introspection: (as defined by Merriam-Webster) observation or examination of one's own mental and emotional state, mental processes, etc.; the act of looking within oneself.

Chapter Nine

Competition

Life is a fight...

You're going be scared you're going to be nervous...

You're going to feel alone in that ring....

You know you're going to get hit, and hit hard.

The real question is will you get back up, knowing life has heavier hits to land...

Will you continues to fight or submit?

See I refuse to allow life to have that on me...

Call it ego, call it survival but I will not allow anything to have...

Oh I see... you rather not even step into that ring, that arena of doubt...

You rather make excuses to why this isn't for you, or you aren't a natural born fighter...

I have news for you, we are born fighting,

You fought trying to get that first breath...

to the moment decided to stand up and walk to fight gravity...

Then you fight to not fall when you started running...

We are all fighters and somewhere in the middle of life you forgot that...

I will be honest, I hate the fight... I hate the anxiety it brings... to feel cornered... is scary...

Hearing the crowd ohhhing and awwwing at every decision made... my life is judged, my relationships weighed... my daily choices are questioned...

Am I a good father? Am I a good husband? Am I as real as I show my self to be... is it an act?

I have been counted out before... I am good at losing... not by choice and when you fight life... you tend to be... but with more loss comes strength... it doesn't ever get better but it does get easier...

I get back up.... I lick my wounds, my cuts turn to scars and I move forward... I learn from my mistakes and find ways of getting stronger.

I know everyone's watching, some are betting for me and some against... they watch every move I make and question every step, they would have done it this way or that.... shoulda coulda wouldas

In the end I know the reasons I fight, I watch them grow as they go through life with fights of their own...

I hope that someday they don't have to take some of the hits I did, I hope their fights are few and far in between... and I hope I have shown them strength so they can overcome anything...

Our only real fight is against ourselves.

This journal entry is one from last year. My whole life I have been training for a fight. Whether it be for my twin sister or to protect this great nation. In all cases the first fight was always within me. I had to beat myself, my own insecurities my own self-doubt first, then I could conquer anything else.

"Competition - There is none. I don't live in the space thinking I am competing with other entertainers. I am always and only competing with myself."

If you are worried about other people's advancements, then you have given yourself barriers.

I have insecurities like how I look in a shirt and my hair line creeping back on the daily, but I don't have positional insecurities. I know where I came from, I know where I am now, and I know where I want to go. Your success will grow when your mindset changes. No one is taking the food out of your mouth. You are taking it out of your own. Stop using your insecurities to enable your boundaries. You can be free of that stress by accepting you are in the position you are in, good or bad. It is solely based on your vision and the boundaries you set for yourself. The Universe rewards hustle.

It often feels like the world is overly consumed by everyone else's life. I can't talk too much shit since its essentially how I got my start into the entertainment industry. The world is fooled by the false face we put on our Instagram and Facebook pages. We are consumed with, and driven by, instant gratification and threatened by anyone trying to advance themselves in the same space. It's an ugly beast. Some would even call it jealousy. I have dealt with this a little in my world, but I haven't let it slow me down. There are too many people in the world looking to make a name for themselves. They do so without remorse or without boundaries of their own dignity. Why is everyone trying to one-up the other? Why do they feel such deep insecurity within themselves? What I am trying to say is, you should be completely confident in what you put out into the world unless you know it's not one-hundred percent genuine. If you know in your heart your life is a facade, then I completely understand why you might always be looking over your shoulder to see if the competition is gaining on you.

On the other hand, imagine that all the things you show to the world are the real and true. Then there would be absolutely no need to hide behind anything. Be honest and real. Why would you feel the need to change if what you are doing in your life is fully how you intend to continue to live your life? If you cannot find happiness in your own skin or in your own being, then you have fallen victim to social expectations and pressures. You are not a genuine participant in your own personal existence. You are a person of circumstance and not a person that is subjective. Meaning, your ideas and actions are based upon someone else's influence, and you are not a free thinker.

You should always strive to improve yourself. You should always be learning. But you should never change your views because you see others who do not share them are more popular. My choice to post my kids and family on social media isn't the most popular idea for people who have a significant following. I have been told to be careful and be smarter. My answer to that is this- I choose to live my life and show my life on my terms. Because I am not only proud of my family, but I also understand that whether I like it or not I am now in a position to be a role model. For those who look up to me, how fair would it be for them if I only showed them the highlights? The simple answer is, it wouldn't be fair. That's not honest, and it is definitely not real.

In my posts I have written blogs and filmed videos of many of my moments of weakness. I do this to build the trust. I am not perfect and never want to ever give off the idea that I am. I am similar to you. I have bills to pay, I have goals I chase, and I have insecurities that I battle every single day. The biggest reason why these don't slow me down is that I can accept that its okay to be flawed. I have no reason to look at another man and envy what he has. I need to look around and work my ass off to get what I want in life. I keep these following guide posts in mind as I navigate the road of social media-

Likes do not equal Validation;

A large following doesn't represent honor;

Don't become a sideshow chasing affirmation from complete strangers.

Why is all this in the competition chapter? Because you are not competing with other people in life. You are competing against yourself!

I opened a barbershop between two other barbershops this year. Outside our door, two blocks to the left and about four blocks to the right are barbershops. I didn't for one second doubt I could become more successful than them. I knew I could at least live and work in the same space with just as much success. I researched their marketing and knew I could provide more. I had more to offer. We may have the same end goal, but the quality of the service provided was much higher, with a cultural goal that was much more profound. We have created a community behind the shop. The shop has a living breathing soul. This is why I wasn't worried about the other shops. I don't see them as competition. I see their presence as motivation. I believe I have better and deeper intentions. With integrity and honesty I would win over enough customers to stay afloat and eventually grow past the others.

If you are competing with others, that means you have set a boundary for your own growth. I don't even acknowledge them anymore. I don't give them the energy to live in my head. They are just other local businesses to me. I simply direct all the effort to becoming great at my venture. I make it a point to run my own race. I won't burden myself with the worry over somebody else's success. I endeavor to grow my own ventures and walk toward my own goals.

Too often, people sell themselves short. They lack vision or they just lack depth. When you have this kind of mindset you have to worry about everyone around you, having to be concerned they might be catching up. Whether they are taking your jobs or if they will be taking your followers should not be worries on your mind.

I hope everyone has success, it is not a zero sum game. I know that's a naive idea, but I still have ideals. People fall victim to their own vanity. They are always looking over their shoulders, wondering who is catching up to them. I refuse to live like that. I would rather keep my head down and plow my way to success. I will always be able to say I did it on my own terms.

You have to evolve, grow, learn, and be malleable enough to adjust your course when necessary. Having the ability to change shapes is important. Not necessarily to conform but to have the ability to shift and drive to improve.

There is only ONE you, so own it. No one has had your life or your experiences. And nobody can appreciate what it is to live in your skin.

So there really is no competition. It is the person who makes it who has beat self-doubt. It can be as easy or as hard as you decide. It is crazy to know you truly are the keeper of your own success or failure.

I deeply believe that I will find more success in helping others find their own success. A rising tide lifts all boats. Think about that. Everyone rising together when something good happens.

If I support a friend and help him get into acting because inadvertently my path led me to an incredible acting opportunity, and he takes that help and becomes the most successful actor in our time, then I have done my part for the greater good. I gave of myself to contribute to his success. Then I am sure he will show the same gratitude for the time when an opportunity opens for someone else, and he will pay his good fortune forward. Live to serve others close to you and build them up without any expectations.

Steve Howie: "I can only open the door. It's up to you to close that door..."

Learn to exist in a place of confidence and self-awareness. Know who you are and what you are capable of doing. That really is all that should matter. You are the sole reason for your success and failures.

For others who view you as their competition, watch with support and without ego. If you have a tool that can help them, offer the hand. If they refuse to take it, they have made the choice out of pride. Their lack of humility will most likely be their biggest downfall.

Your success will grow when your mindset changes. No one is taking the food out of your mouth. You are taking it out of your own. Stop using your insecurities to enable your boundaries. You can be free of that stress by accepting you are in the position you are in, be it good or bad, solely based on your vision and the boundaries you set for yourself.

It's not easy to just focus on your work when you see others having major success. It's actually hard to remain composed and stay the course. It's easy to join the masses by selling yourself short to in order to copy others. But it is not honorable. Misery and discontent also readily accompany these mindsets and attitudes, so it's critical to steer clear.

Be the slow burn. Don't be something you know will get you immediate attention. But the casual change that motivates others to do the same. Lead by being a solid example to those around you. It will not always go unnoticed. The universe rewards hustle.

Now don't get me wrong, competition is generally a good thing. It forces most of us to push ourselves and do our best. Whereas when there is no competition, it renders the person into complacency and leaves them satisfied with mediocre. That isn't ever going to work for me. If I'm in, I'm all in. Half-ass on anything is never acceptable in my world. I set my bar higher everyday, and kill myself trying to reach it. And when I get close, I raise it again. Constantly moving the objective is the only thing I find that keeps me sharp and hungry to achieve more everyday.

I've been competing all my life, and honestly at this point, I am pretty sure I would miss it if it were gone. But I am not into the outright bloodsport anymore. I realize now more than ever that success isn't a zero sum total game. And we can all help each other as we travel the long road to success. Sure, some people are going to quit along the way. Hard work tends to weed those quitters out pretty quickly. And we all know that we are each better than some people, but there is always someone better than us. So just run your own race, be a good dude, and help others where you can. It isn't going to take away from your success when you lend a hand to someone in need. It will make your victory all the sweeter because it didn't come at the cost of others. And that will make you not only happy, but proud.

Do you ever notice horses run their fastest when they have other horses to run against and overtake? If you don't know this, try observing if you ever get the chance. When you are solo on horseback you can ride hell for leather for a good amount of time depending on the fitness of the horse. But get a friend or someone else on a mount next to you? You would never have known horses love to race as much as humans love it. They chase and pursue and push themselves to overtake their competition. But they return to the paddock and eat and hang out together no matter which was faster. We don't need to worry over what others are doing or accomplishing. Knowing that you gave it everything you had to whatever your endeavor was that day, should be enough to let you sleep soundly that night. Don't leave anything on the table of life. Leave it all out there for the sake of pushing yourself and nobody else to get to the next level. We are our only competition.

facade: (as defined by Merriam-Webster)- a false, superficial, or artificial appearance or effect.

Chapter Ten

Gratitude - Humility - Death

We are not broken nor are we singular individuals, we have experienced levels of life that many will not do or even dare to do. This actually makes us the complete opposite of broken, we are well put together, we have adapted and converted our originally vulnerable and innocent beings into a callused form of experience. We are a better put together human. A more completed system that can withstand hardships. If used in the proper manner we can accomplish unbelievable acts. We can live a fulfilled life, but only when we acknowledge the fact that what we went through made us complete. It made us ready to take on the world.

I wrote this journal entry to identify that our experiences make us special, we are not victims to our lives. If you continue to view hardships as a personal attack, you will always be held down with fear and suffering. But if you view it as a learning experience, the scar can tell one hell of a story.

I t's almost an oxymoron for me to talk about being humble. Insert 'LOL' and laughing emoji here. This is how I see things. People often use the description "self-made" when they describe the success of a person that had some set of odds stacked against them. I personally can't say with any degree of conviction that I am self-made. I have had hundreds of minds carve my path for me. I have learned from and listened to some of the best and worst in life.

This is how I do most things in life, I walk into the room and listen. I hear the conversation, I learn from the room full of wisdom before I open up and speak, metaphorically and physically. My life is nothing but lessons learned from the rest of the world. I give all the credit to everyone else. My mom, dad, brothers, sisters, friends, strangers, and enemies. I have learned from everyone. So, people call me humble? I think it is actually more of my gratitude that just takes the form of humility. I appreciate my life and the life that has been provided for my family. But I also do not just live to provide for my family. I live to provide for everyone. I have spent so many years learning from the world, I want to make myself available for others to learn from me. Be that my life of mistakes, or the lessons learned, take your pick.

If you asked me the questions a year ago or even two years ago; are you full? Are you happy? Can you go peacefully into the night? The answers then would be an unequivocal, "No." But today I am happy. I am proud now of what I have done in my life. My kids will be proud of my legacy. My wife would be hurt, of course, because in our marriage she wants to be the one to go out first. But I believe she would be able to speak proudly of her husband and the man he was, on and off social media. I can say I have achieved what I set out to do. It's a blessing that I am still doing it.

A strange sense of insecurity washes over me, with no reason and no explanation. I think back and remember a poem I wrote a while back.

Everyone sees me stand tall, but inside you wouldn't believe how small I really feel...

They see a genuine smile and hear a soulful laugh, but I hear the cries of a soul that feels alone.

You can see me, but do you really see me?

Do you see how my life isn't always easy?

How my friends confide in me, how I give every breath to everyone around me?

Some who ask how I am, aren't the ones who should really

care...

Family just expects me to get through, little do they know I am barely holding on...

It's a tight rope balancing act with a smile on my face...

You only see one side of this eclipse because darkness isn't a pretty face.

I hold myself up, because my bones are strong, but my spirit isn't what my body portrays.

I can use a compliment... or two, but is it an insecurity to reach for love, to beg for affirmation?

But damn, don't you think I deserve that every once in a while? Don't you think I earned it?

I act selfless, but I am always looking over my shoulder for some sign of appreciation.

I can't help it, this is me. Am I needy, or am I human? Am I broken and just need the right touch? Or am I just tired of doing too much?

I feel like I have so much depth, I have so many sides, and maybe that's why I never feel fulfilled.

Deep you say?

Well, I wish I was shallow... not in the sense you are thinking, but in the sense of being easy to fill.

I don't get why I am needing love, needing a touch or maybe

a hug. It's something I need, to be able to hold onto at a time I feel like I am falling...

One finger after another keeps losing grip, I can only hold on for so long.

"Shake this feeling, you are better than this,

pick your head up and smile because everyone expects it."

"Smile and wave, smile and wave"

Look at my perfect life on Facebook, look at how happy I am.

'Keep smiling kid you have them all fooled'

Stand up tall and walk proud.

I carry the weight of one man and it's more than the world will understand.

How long can I keep up this pace? When will I be done with this race? All I want to be is a good man...

I make mistakes but do the best I honestly can with just a promise to keep waking up, trying, and to be a good man.

The truth is I want to do more. I have been setting up to do more for the world around me. But as of now, if my story were laid out for others to read or to watch, I do not know if they would learn from my mistakes. I am not sure if they would be inspired by my thoughts. I also don't know whether or not I have helped make a small footprint of change on this earth. I feel like the answer to all those is a resounding 'yes.' And if it is not a 'yes' now, I hope to make it an undeniable 'yes' in the future.

Life tends to ferret out a way of humbling us all at some point or another. I have always had the mindset to not allow life to throw surprise parties for me. Meaning, I do what I can to expect the unexpected. I take the time to 'war-game' life. I am prepared for the worst but always hope for the best. I have played every scenario out in my head. Sure, it's dark at times, but this is what I put myself through to be ready for anything.

Life won't control my emotions. I will.

I just can't allow life to try and bring me down. So, I stay humble and never expect more than I should. For instance filming this TV show, people ask me all the time if I am excited. The answer is, "yes and no." Yes, because this could be the beginning of a new branch on my life and a new page in my book. But I am also indifferent. I am forced to ask myself if the show bombs, will it ruin me? Fuck no, because I always played the possibility out in my head before I even started it.

Perspective. The word and concept take on a whole new meaning with the signing of a document agreeing you understand the worst-case scenario of this procedure is death. Death. Let me help you understand where my life was at that time. I went through a divorce and was back to being a single father. I was ready to do it on my own forever. Let's be straight, no one is proud to have two divorces under their belt by the ripe old age of thirty-five.

My parents have been married for forty-three years. To say I wasn't disappointed in myself was an understatement. But here we were, a thirty-five year old single father of four kids, struggling to know what my next moves in life would be. I made a dramatic decision by leaving the border patrol to pursue a business and entertainment career, but that wasn't exactly a proper structure for my kids. And the problems were doubled since being a single father hurt my ability to travel for work.

By the grace of God and with extreme hesitation I met the most incredible woman. We were both in our thirties. We both had kids. And both of us, deep in our hearts, just wanted to have what we had growing up. A family. So why the hesitation? If I didn't attempt to have another relationship, then I wouldn't ever have the possibility of another divorce. That fact alone was so significant in contributing to my hesitation. The fear was there but our relationship was so different from what I had known until her. It felt right. Possibly it felt rushed, but at the same time it seemed almost needed.

When we first started talking, I was tired of searching for this dream relationship where I could just live happily ever after. I wasn't sure if it existed, and I was getting tired of wasting time with others to find out it was time I could have given to someone else. I asked three simple questions. How old are you? Do you have kids? What do you do for a living? She was confused on the direct questions but then I explained to her, I don't need more friends and I am not looking for a hook up, I want something more. I was a single father who still believed in the values of raising a family. I knew that age was important in determining whether she was ready to settle down. And I felt someone with kids would be able to understand how to treat them, as well as understand the stress of being a parent. She answered without hesitation and asked me the same questions back. From there it was smooth sailing.

Four months later, there we were in the hospital. My stubborn ass didn't want to go in to get checked, until it got to the point where I was so weak I could not even walk ten feet without having to stop and catch my breath. It was scary, and I will be honest, I was concerned. They wanted me to get into an ambulance I politely refused. Hard-headed as always, I got in the car and we drove to the hospital. We were halfway to the hospital when I had to pull over and let my wife drive the rest of the way. By the time she got me there they were waiting and ready to receive me.

I had to stay in the hospital for four miserable days. A-fib is a condition where the heart beats at an irregular rhythm. This means the blood isn't flowing normally and can, in that case, pool and coagulate which may potentially cause a stroke. That's cool, right? So there we were, addressing the first issue which was to lower my heart rate. My heart was basically working at a dead sprint for four days. The most immediate fear is having a sudden cardiac arrest.

The medical team pushed medication to try and regulate it while they ran a series of tests to see if they could get my heart to return to a normal rhythm. They also started a few rounds of blood thinners as a precaution. Once the doctors felt they were ready for the procedure, off we went. An echo cardio-gram and a cardio-version (closer look into the heart to see if there are any clots and then ride the lightning) were taken as they were wheeling me to the room. With my wife walking alongside me and holding my hand, I got emotional.

While I was in the hospital my wife would go home to take care of the kids, shower, and change her clothes. My mother-in-law was there helping us for the time being. The first night of my wife's return to the hospital, she handed me a jar of notes from the kids. They got together and decided to send me little notes of encouragement.

They all read something different.

"I love you."

"You are the best dad ever."

"Please get better soon."

"I miss you."

While I write this even now, I get emotional to know that my kids were feeling as much confusion as I was. I hate that they felt the needed to write those notes, but it was definitely an awakening for me that they did.

I couldn't help but think, "Lord, I need you here." (whatever your religious beliefs are, it's not my business) I tend to always resort back to training when I'm truly afraid and out of my depth, like when I was in Iraq. "Dear Lord, I know we haven't seen eye to eye since I was six, but I am asking for a little help today. My daughter is being born soon and I would love to be there for that." And here I was again, praying to the big man for some assistance. "Lord, it would suck to lose this beautiful life that I have only had a short chance to enjoy. I finally have my children, my wife, and the family I have always wanted. I would love some more time. I just need more time..."

My mother and wife then said their potential last good-bye's.

Strictly speaking in medical terms, the odds of

someone dying from this procedure are very low. But there was a chance, and I wasn't ready.

I fell asleep and woke up in normal rhythm.

That moment changed me.

I walked away from anything I felt wasn't in my best interest and was wasting my time, because the only time I wanted was more with my new little family. I resolved to continue this practice going forward.

It gave me the extra push to keep moving forward with my dream and all my goals. I committed to help more and do more. This incident made me appreciate what I have right in front of me. It also forced me to question what I have not focused on, but should have.

I started focusing on myself. I was focusing on my health, yes. But I was also focused on my circle, my world.

My mantra became: be a better father, be a better husband, be a better person.

Facing death isn't exactly a fun way to spend your days.

It's a crazy feeling, lying in a hospital bed feeling my heart beat and knowing it's off. Everyone in the room is comfortable with the situation. It is something they see from time to time. The best-case scenario is that the heart goes back into normal rhythm with the medications given.

Worst-case scenario is death, but that's rare, they say. Since it is not their emergency, it basically feels like they don't really care.

I smile and sign the papers. I'm feeling good about the odds but still wondering at the thought, what if I am in that one percent? Will this be the last time I see my kids? Was that last moment with them a positive one? Was it one they can hold onto when they feel lost and I am no longer there to guide them? Have you imagined this feeling? War-gaming life, and war-gaming death.

A patch on my chest and a patch on my back. Anticipation of the shock, knowing it's coming and anticipating death as I am contemplating my life...

I don't normally fear death, but I know how hard it would be for my family to be spontaneously left without a father and a husband. I can feel their pain and it terrifies me to consider leaving them this way.

Life is such a fragile experience. Yet we often treat it as if it is bullet proof. We fight it. We don't listen to it. We refuse to figure out how to best work in it.

It leads me to question everything. I hope I did enough. I hope I made them proud.

"I am going to push the button."

I don't feel the lift, but I feel the fall.

I feel heat throughout my body and it feels like it exited through my toes. I hear myself scream as if I fear death has taken over. Then I start hearing voices around me.

"His rhythm is normal" reaches my ears from a faraway voice.

I am still here. I will have another chance.

What do I need to change and what needs to remain?

The pain medication wears off...

I have life to look forward to now. I need to fix what needs fixing and get it right.

I have not always been this guy. I wasn't anyone the world would even think twice to look at or even follow. I can almost pinpoint the exact moment I turned an idea into my new life motto.

In Kentucky I was lost, stuck living in a place that never felt like home. I repeatedly asked myself, why do I do this? And why don't I change it?

It wasn't long after that I was in the military and living a new life. I have never been an emotional man. My father was my example of a man and he has never shed a tear in front of me. He doesn't show much sympathy for anything, really. A loving man with rough edges, that's how I think of him. I always wished I were more like him.

I can remember the moment I felt broken because my friend was killed in training. He was someone who had become close to me. I remember fighting the tears for most of the day, and then I opened the door to my apartment. As the door opened and I walked in, I knew I could hide from the world and I was now allowed to show emotions. The tears fell as I sobbed, the kind of crying where you have a strange quiver in your breathing, a genuine hurt and confusion. This was my first friend in the military who had lost his life. I think it was more painful knowing it was in training and a site I was on just days prior, doing the same training.

I couldn't catch my breath. It was confusing because I didn't know where all these emotions came from, as if I were watching myself and thinking, what's happening to me? Get it together Vince.

This wasn't how a man was supposed to act. It wasn't the example my father set for me.

I felt so much after this. I remember kicking my first dead body in Afghanistan. It's something I was taught. I had done it in training hundreds of times. But when I did it there, in the theater of war and death, it took the wind out of me. The body was... hard. I guess I really didn't expect that. I don't know what I expected, it's hard to explain. It was as if he turned to stone and it messed with my head.

Maybe that was how my mind chose to deal with it. I coped by removing anything human about it and fantasized a different reality in my own head.

I turned and signaled to an NCO with a nod, "he's dead." We both already knew, but maybe it was a moment of relief at a second opinion.

I guess at that point I had seen so much pain, and I had experienced so much life in my twenties, that it changed me. I wasn't the man I am today. Small parts of that man exist, but the rest is new. I see life now, and I feel it completely.

I have seen death and what it does to the families when their loved ones are killed in action, lost from illness, died in training, or even dead by their own hands. I have been there.

I have been there while mothers are crying and their kids are confused by daddy's makeup as he lays in the open casket. I have watched the fiancée who never got that chance to marry the man of her dreams, pulling his body halfway out the casket to get one last good hug. The father that mentions I remind him of his fallen son breaks my heart still today. The mother who said I smelled just like her son leaves me haunted. I have seen the marriage that never seems to get back to good after a son chose to take his own life, while the parents berate themselves and their failures.

I am blessed and haunted by all these moments. I have been equipped with the ability to endure the damage and keep going. With a high rebound rate and resilience despite the vivid memories, I go forward. I feel empathy. So much so that it crushes me, because it stirs up the past and I live the pain I see in others eyes. I feel myself reliving my own pain and I know what they are going through.

Continuing to push myself to be a good person is my baseline, being the best person I can be because I know those struggles. I know addiction and depression. I feel the world and everyone's pain. I guess death has been that one humbling factor that no one can avoid. It's the truth that waits for us all. From birth to death you can see life as a distracted existence or an opportunity to make an impact.

I care so much about leaving a positive impact on this world to help others find their calling, I find I can neglect myself. I know that leaving a blue print of a life full of mistakes can help guide others to success. If one person can take any lesson from my collection of mistakes, then making them has not been in vain. This life doesn't have to be harder than it already is.

I felt compelled to write this book because I look at my life right now and never in a million years did I think I would be doing this. A small part of me somewhere deep in my mind, believed I was meant to live a life that would always serve others. I was meant to be in this world to accomplish something meaningful, and live with purpose.

I still believe I haven't fulfilled that calling. But, if you looked at my life ten years ago, you wouldn't call me an inspiration. You wouldn't say, "That's a man I would aspire to be." You wouldn't say, "I want to be like him some day."

Something changed in me, something so profound that it has shaped the man I am today. Maybe I was writing this to help you put your life in perspective. It's not too late to start changing your stars.

I have started and been traveling the journey of changing mine. And now I hope to help others do the same. The best thing is, I've already made all the mistakes and fucked up more than most people can imagine. But I came back. I fought hard. I continue to show up for the fight day after day because when we stop fighting we might as well die. I will not stop fighting. My family and giving back to this world mean too much to me.

So here are a few of my pearls neatly summed up.

Not happy? Change it.

Death is just as much a part of life as birth.

A sentence can end with a period, a question mark, or

an exclamation point. Choose how you want it to end, or let it run on. It's your story.

Facing disappointment, adversity, anger, anxiety, struggle, conflict, fear, and death... All of these are unavoidable and imminent facts of life. How you take and deal with, or respond to, them, and sorting out the rest will determine how you function in the world.

Happiness is yours to pluck from the ether, so go get it. Nothing is stopping you except your own imagination.

I struggled through so many things for so many years that it's almost laughable. I sometimes think my life would make a good movie. Whether it would be a comedy, a tragedy, a horror story, or an action flick really depends on the day. The awesome benefit to having lived through the things I have, is that I have some useful wisdom and experiences to pass forward now. I'm blessed in more ways than I can count, and give thanks for those blessings every single day. That's a practice I can't recommend enough for people to do. Give thanks for what you have, it will help you get closer to what you want. And remember that life isn't always about having what you want, but wanting what you've got. If I touch just one life with the words on these pages, then it was worth every minute of the work it took to write it. Maybe you know someone it might help. It would be my honor if you passed it forward and encouraged them to seek the encouragement within these pages.

There is an old parable about the lighthouse and the tugboat. I'm not going to launch into an entire novel telling it back to you, but I can paraphrase. It is safe to say, this is one of the life lessons that kind of blows your mind when you first hear it. And like anything else, you can take what applies to you and leave the rest. The important thing, is that you consider it.

The parable describes how a tugboat and a lighthouse do the very same job, just in two different ways. The tugboat brings ships into the harbor safely by pushing, pulling, and towing them. This of course takes a whole lot of effort, and even more energy. They are responsible for moving a vessel that may be twenty times larger than the tugboat itself. That actually sounds like an impossible task when you think about it in simple terms. But for the entire era of the tugboat, they have made this crazy feat of physics happen.

The lighthouse also brings ships safely into the harbor. They guide the vessels in a way that avoids rocky shallows or other water hazards that may sink them. Imagine the disaster that would no doubt ensue, if the lamp of a lighthouse in a busy harbor were doused. The damage would be catastrophic. So, the human element ensures the light is never out, so that human life will be preserved.

What does all of that mean? Well, the simple fact is that I spent a hell of long time being the tugboat. I pushed at life. I pulled at the adversities. I towed my responsibilities. I saved lives when and where I COULD, and when they NEEDED saving. I struggled with the daily existence. I struggled with obligations. I spent huge amounts of energy on things that required my effort. I exhausted myself and my limited fuel reserves when I needed to save my own life. There wasn't really a time that I doubted I needed to do all these things. I am naturally one who wants to help the people around me. I believe that this is a quality that can't really be taught to anyone. Some people just naturally have it, and sometimes people are put here to serve other purposes. It's best if you find out early in life which of these you are, it will save you a whole lot of energy and heartache.

Now, at this point in my life, I like to think I'm much more like the lighthouse. I live to care for others and help those who need it. Being a guiding light may sound like a cheesy idea to some people. But to me, it is my life's purpose. To be the light toward which lost vessels steer; to avoid hazards, danger, and certain disaster. I can't think of a greater honor that others would give me than to let me be their light, and take my wisdom and experience, and apply it in their own lives. To use that guidance to help bring them happiness, success, or just inner peace.

Maybe, I can help you work harder at maintaining your work-life balance. Finding a way to spend more time nurturing your family and other relationships in your life will never be something you regret. While NOT doing that, and focusing on accumulating more wealth and success, will definitely make you feel regret. No man has, "If only I had spent more time at work" carved on his tombstone. Maybe, I can help you get past the loss of a friend whose life was lost too early. Bringing you to the conclusion that they would want you to be happy, healthy, and fulfilled on the earth they had to leave too soon.

Maybe you're feeling like hope is lost, and you are being weighed down by something, by anything. And after reading through here, maybe you're able to realize that when everything looks hopeless, you still can summon your strength and ask for help. Everything is never totally hopeless, until you decide it is. So decide to always keep going. Decide to change your mind. Decide to change your path, because it isn't carved in stone. John Lennon once said, "everything will be okay in the end. If it's not okay, it's not the end." There is always a bit of hope to be had, and a way out. Even when in a moment of chaos, we may feel we are sinking fast, there is still a chance. The great thing is, the sun will still rise in the morning. And a new day will greet you with the sun, with another chance to change your life for the better. A new opportunity to right whatever went wrong the day before, is now in front of you. What are you going to do with it?

I have been fighting for most of my life. I have the scars and stories to prove it. I have also competed during my life. But, I've never been one to be so caught up in a win or loss that I let it define me. It isn't about winning, this beautiful life. It's about wanting to win. It's about never giving up. Having the courage to never quit and to soldier on, no matter what comes your way, that is what it's all about.

They say that your life isn't the two dates on your tombstone. Your life is the dash in-between them. How do you want your dash to be lived? No matter what you want that dash to represent, make it yours. No matter where you are on the path of your life, you can ALWAYS make a turn. A turn for the better, a turn to go another way, or even a U-turn can be made whenever you choose. Your life is whatever you decide to make it. And that, my friends, is a beautiful thing.

Post Scripts

This is a late entry, and when I say late I mean just days before this went to print- I wanted to add this.

I feel guilty in a serious way for not reaching out to my military buddy when I had been telling myself I needed to call him. Danny Reetz died November 5th, 2018, from the injuries he sustained in a tragic motorcycle accident. I met Danny two years ago when I went to Texas A&M to speak to a group of veterans about transition. He mentioned going through some struggles and was now going to school and getting his shit together. He would send random messages of encouragement my way and pushed me to keep doing the work. He believed in me. It was incredibly inspiring to receive these messages. Whether he was three sheets to the wind, or in the gym getting his pump on, his message was always nothing but encouragement. I have always been appreciative of the extra effort he put into our friendship and, I have always taken the time to reciprocate that love. I told myself I would give him more time. I told myself out of all the people who are in my circle, he is one of the guys who deserves more time. And with a heavy heart as I write this, I am mad at myself for not making good on that idea. It sat in my head, and I let it poke at me for too long before making the decision to act.

Life is so fragile...

I can't believe it. My own words of encouragement could have been so powerful, if my dear friend would have slowed down just a little, and listened to the concern in my requests. I can't be so vain as to believe my thoughts could have swayed his beliefs enough to take a few more precautionary steps. My friend was an amazing man who was hard to slow down. Some would say he flew faster then his angels could follow. I would say he flew with the angels, leading them to save more souls such as myself. Danny, I waited too long to say I love you, brother. Until we ride again...

I will forever pay more attention to that voice. I will make more of an effort to reach out, because none of us know when those few words of encouragement can motivate another to be great, or be just enough to keep someone going.

As a dyslexic whose first full book ever read all the way through was in 2003, at the age of twenty-three years old when I was in Afghanistan. Until recently, I hadn't known the difference between there, their and they're. I became aware of the proper use of 'too' a few years prior. I still can't tell the difference from a lower case b or d, because my brain doesn't recognize the difference. I write in all caps and my biggest fear about finishing this book is that people will ask me to sign it for them. I write like a five year-old and spell like a three year-old.

We will always seek truth and happiness. They are universal values we will always naturally desire. I believe the answer to that is knowing who you are and what you represent. Being content comes from being honest. Honest with yourself, and honest with the world looking upon us.

So here I am, thirty-eight years-old, married for the third time, and finally feeling it's right, raising six kids with whom I try to be stern but fair, also knowing there are times I am quick to yell instead of teach. I have one son who blames my first divorce on me, and doesn't seem to want to let that go. A daughter who just started dating and I am trying to find comfort in that idea. I have another son with the same reading disorder I had, and nothing kills me more than knowing what he's going through, and wishing I could take that struggle away from him. I have struggles with managing money, I have issues with getting back in shape. I am not in a place where I myself can say I am successful with any level of conviction. I strive to find balance still. I can tell you this. I have at least been able to acknowledge my short comings and how they affect my life directly and how to start working to better myself. And I live firmly comforted in the belief, that you can do it too.

This is another of my story-type journal entries that set me toward writing a book. I guess you could say this was the idea that set the plan in motion. I love writing, I always have. But my lifelong struggle with dyslexia has kept me from being able to properly tell all the stories that are trapped in my mind. But I didn't want to be stopped by this disability. I found a way. I practiced. I wrote, and wrote some more. I found some help. And once I found the right help, I was able to fully bring this book to life. Don't be afraid to ask for help. You have so much ability, and it's a shame to waste it. Help is around, you just need to ask.

Each morning when I was a kid, I'd lace up my sneakers and hit the ground running.

My personal creed has always consisted of one goal: When I lace 'em up in the morning, I want to be excited and passionate about what I'm doing every day.

It's funny; I always knew it was a privilege even to have boots to lace up. It wasn't necessarily anything someone said to me, I just had an innate awareness of how lucky I was at a young age. I had a general concept that there were other people in the world who didn't have as much as I did, and I was genuinely appreciative of my blessings.

For example, we'd go to Mexico twice a year, and my mom would always give me some money to buy chiclets from kids on the street.

But I didn't need any damn chiclets, and I knew it. So I'd just give all the money to the kids and let them keep their inventory. I felt how lucky I was not to be selling gum on the streets. I deeply felt it.

Whether you call it sympathy or empathy for others, I was born with it. I could look into other people's eyes and, feel.

Feel their pain. Their sadness. Their joy. Their hurt.

I knew my mission in life was to help others. Somehow. Some way.

But it didn't mean I wouldn't veer from that path – intentionally or not.

Each morning when I was in high school and college, I'd lace up my cleats and hit the ground running.

Literally.

I've been an athlete all my life, and baseball was my passion. I loved every second of it. The smell of the grass, the history of the game and the camaraderie of my teammates. It's a special game.

I loved baseball so much, if fact, that over time my focus shifted from others to myself.

In a way, it kind of had to. The amount of work athletes put in – along with the time honing their craft – doesn't typically allow for altruism on a daily basis (or so I thought).

I thought I was invincible. It wasn't until I became academically ineligible to play in college that reality slapped me across the face.

What the hell are you doing? I thought. You're 21, can't finish college, there is no plan to continue pursuing baseball, no income and you have a kid on the way.

At that point, the only solution I could think of was joining the military.

Each morning when I was an Army Ranger, I'd lace up my boots and hit the ground running.

When I made the decision to serve, I essentially made up my mind that I was going to die in combat.

However, I was 100-percent fine with that.

Why? Well, if that happened, it would mean two things:

1. That I'd no longer be a selfish prick.

2. My daughter would benefit from the insurance, and I'd be a hero.

But a funny thing happened; I didn't die.

Not on my first deployment. Or my second. Or my third.

I truly thought my purpose was gone. Once again, I knew I was meant to help others, but at this point, I was out of ideas to fulfill that drive.

I kept searching for answers. Through working as a corrections officer to joining the border patrol.

I knew I was doing something good, but I still didn't feel it.

I was looking outside of myself to justify my existence.

Each morning when I get up to make a video, I put on my slippers and hit the ground running.

Slippers, by the way, are fucking AWESOME.

I'm incredibly fortunate to be in a position now to help others who are struggling. That's what my mission is. Along with being a father and husband, it's my life's work.

Here's the thing: It doesn't matter what kind of fucking shoes you have or don't have. I don't care if it's sneakers, cleats, boots or slippers – lace 'em up, find your passion and stick with it.

There is no "mold" for your life; every single person is different. It's YOUR life!

I believe fear and worry are the only enemies of mankind; don't fear what other people think of you and certainly don't worry about following the path everyone else took.

That's their path. Not yours.

There is nothing I'm going through that other people aren't. Like you, I've had countless "rock bottoms." I don't have all the answers. I'm not perfect. But what I do have is an insatiable desire to do better.

Better than I was in college. Better than I was in the Army.

A better father. A better husband.

Shit, better than I was 15 minutes ago.

Ultimately, that's all we can ask of ourselves as men and women.

You're going to fuck up; it's bound to happen from time to time.

Do better...

You'll say the wrong thing at the absolute wrong time.

Do better...

You'll choose not to help someone you are fully capable of helping.

Do better...

Just be yourself, man...

And when you lace up your boots, hit the ground running.

Acknowledgements

I have a few brief thanks I need to extend to some important people who not only are instrumental in my life, but are my heartbeat. Thank you all, for either being a brick in my foundation or making an impact in getting it built.

To my Wife- my road dog, my friend. Thank you for supporting me on the nights I didn't sleep and the mornings I woke up too early. You can now catch up on cuddle time... until my next book...

If today be the day that I die, at least let it be in your arms, my last gesture will be to take a deep breath and hold it, so I can take as much of you as I can with me as I go...-written for my amazing wife before I went in to get my heart shocked.

To my Kids - For being the motivation that drives me to leave a legacy that I can be proud of.

To my Father - For giving me an example of what a man should be, and at a level I am still trying to achieve.

To my Mother - For being the rock and hammer of the Vargas household.

Jim Danials - Who taught me something so simple yet profound I still find comfort in it. "Home is where you lay your hat."

Post Malone - For supplying the music that made writing flow out of my brain.

Vanessa - The best twin sister a man can have... Thank you for renting me the back left corner of your table while I wrote this book.

To lonely nights in Owensboro Kentucky - This is the exact location I realized I can change my path... Motivation and sacrifice would be needed.

Ben York - Thank you for seeing something more in me... for the edits and the motivation in writing.

To Anthony, Hector, Lamar, and Doug - Miss you boys... Time isn't slowing down! Let's find time to see each other.

To the man I gave an Uber ride - You said you could see the future and you saw I would be extremely successful. Thanks for that. Still waiting, but hopeful.

Luke - Thank you for trusting in me. I am not done yet...

Kendra Middleton Williams - Thank you, for believing in me and trusting that I had a story worth telling.

SSG Barraza and SGT Brehm - Your influence pours through me for others to follow. This is because of your dedication to the mission and country. I only hope I have made you proud.

Devin - Dec 16, 2005 -You earned your tab on the day I did. You were my motivation.

"God arms me with strength,
and He makes my way perfect.
He makes me as surefooted as a deer,
enabling me to stand on mountain heights.
He trains my hands for battle;
He strengthens my arm to draw a bronze bow.
You have given me Your shield of victory.
Your right hand supports me;
Your help has made me great."

This moment I take to offer my humble gratitude to God Almighty, for this life is His gift to me. And for all the gifts I've been given, and all the times He has saved my life, I vow I will never waste another day not living for Him. Grateful, humble, and appreciative always to the One who grants me life and all my blessings on this earth, every single day. -Vincent

Made in the USA
San Bernardino, CA
23 November 2018